REMAKING THE ANC

REMAKING THE ANC

Party Change in South Africa and the Global South

edited by Anthony Butler

First published by Jacana Media (Pty) Ltd in 2014

10 Orange Street
Sunnyside
Auckland Park 2092
South Africa
+2711 628 3200
www.jacana.co.za

© The authors, 2014

All rights reserved. No part of this book may be reproduced or utilised in any form and by any means, electronic or mechanical, including photocopying, without permission in writing from the publisher.

ISBN 978-1-4314-2019-3

Cover design by Shawn Paikin and Maggie Davey
Set in Bembo 11/14pt
Printed and bound by Creda Communications
Job no. 002303

See a complete list of Jacana titles at www.jacana.co.za

Contents

Preface vii
List of contributors ix

1. Introduction: Understanding party adaptation
   Anthony Butler 1
2. The organisational learning of the Kuomintang in democratic
   Taiwan *Alexander Tan* 14
3. Mexico's Institutional Revolutionary Party: Reform
   and resurgence *Kenneth F. Greene & Hector Ibarra-Rueda* 29
4. Power, patronage and politics in Malaysia: UMNO's
   dominant state? *Edmund Terence Gomez* 52
5. The Workers' Party of Brazil: The pragmatic trap
   Guilherme Simões Reis 69
6. Information and communications technology and the
   transformation of the Chinese Communist Party
   Ping Shum & Zheng Yongnian 84

7. Factional dynamics in the Indian National Congress and
   the African National Congress *Thiven Reddy* 101
8. Party–state relations in South Africa in a period of transition
   Vinothan Naidoo 121
9. The idea of organisational renewal in the African National
   Congress *Heidi Brooks Yung* 137
10. Which future for the African National Congress?
    Anthony Butler 157
Notes 169
Index 191

Preface

It has been a real pleasure to prepare this book. The local authors were enthused by the intellectual energy and wisdom of our colleagues from other continents. Our discussions together have shed fresh light on the challenges confronting South Africa's governing party.

The study would not have been possible without the assistance of the Friedrich Ebert Stiftung. I am especially grateful to the former FES resident director Axel Schmidt and to his successor Renate Tenbusch for their enthusiasm and support. Sindy Mtembu and Romi Reineke were efficient and accommodating programme managers.

Russell Martin at Jacana has been a wonderful editor. Stephen Louw from the University of the Witwatersrand and Matthijs Bogaards from Jacobs University in Bremen reviewed the chapters and provided valuable feedback for the authors and editor. I am grateful to Julia Jellema-Butler for compiling the index with her usual unfailing efficiency.

Anthony Butler
Cape Town

Contributors

Anthony Butler is Professor of Political Studies at the University of Cape Town. He has been a Fellow of Emmanuel College, Cambridge; Director of the Politics and Administration Programme at Birkbeck College, University of London; and Chair in Political Studies at the University of the Witwatersrand. Butler's research focuses on politics and public policy in South Africa. He is the author of five books, most recently *The Idea of the ANC*.

Edmund Terence Gomez is Professor of Political Economy at the Faculty of Economics and Administration, University of Malaya. He has also held appointments at the University of Leeds (UK) and Murdoch University (Australia) and served as Visiting Professor at Kobe University, Japan, and at the School of Political Science, University of Michigan. His publications include *Malaysia's Political Economy: Politics, Patronage and Profits*.

Kenneth Greene is Associate Professor in the Department of Government at the University of Texas at Austin. His research focuses on authoritarian regimes, democratisation, political parties, elections and voting behaviour. His book *Why Dominant Parties Lose: Mexico's Democratization in Comparative Perspective* was awarded the 2008 Best

Book Award from the Comparative Democratization Section of the APSA.

Hector Ibarra-Rueda is a specialist in comparative politics and research methodology. His 2013 PhD dissertation, 'Why Factions Matter: A Theory of Party Dominance at the Subnational Level', completed at the University of Texas at Austin, explored the implications of democratisation for unity in dominant parties.

Vinothan Naidoo is Senior Lecturer in the Department of Political Studies at the University of Cape Town. His recent publications explore anti-corruption enforcement in South Africa, the challenges of policy coordination at programme level, and expenditure volatility in provincial government.

Ping Shum is a PhD candidate at the National University of Singapore–King's College London Joint Degree Programme. His central research interest is the Chinese Communist Party's Internet propaganda strategies. Ping has ten years of experience in journalism, including seven years at the BBC in London, where he worked at the Chinese version of the BBC News online.

Thiven Reddy is Senior Lecturer in the Department of Political Studies at the University of Cape Town. His book *Hegemony and Resistance: Contesting Identities in South Africa* draws on the writings of Gramsci and Foucault to theorise the construction of identity in South Africa. He was awarded a Commonwealth Fellowship to Bristol University in 2001 and the Harvard–Mandela Fellowship in 2003.

Guilherme Simões Reis is Professor in the Federal University of the State of Rio de Janeiro. His PhD dissertation explored contemporary social democracy in Europe and South America. He has been a researcher in the South American Political Observer (OPSA) and in the Group of Studies on Congress (NECON).

CONTRIBUTORS

Alex Tan is Professor of Political Science at the University of Canterbury (Christchurch, New Zealand), Senior Fellow at the John G. Tower Center for Political Studies at Southern Methodist University (Dallas, Texas, US), and Research Associate of the Election Study Center at National Chengchi University (Taiwan). He has published numerous books and academic articles in the areas of comparative political parties and elections, comparative political economy, international affairs, Taiwan politics, East Asian politics and European politics.

Zheng Yongnian is Professor and Director of the East Asian Institute, National University of Singapore. He is the author of 13 books, including *Technological Empowerment*, *De Facto Federalism in China*, *Discovering Chinese Nationalism in China* and *Globalization and State Transformation in China*, and coeditor of 11 books on China's politics and society. He served as a consultant to the United Nations Development Programme on China's rural development and democracy. He has also been a columnist for *Xinbao* (Hong Kong) and *Zaobao* (Singapore) for many years, writing numerous commentaries on China's domestic and international affairs.

Heidi Brooks Yung is a PhD candidate in political studies at the University of the Witwatersrand in Johannesburg. Her research interests are democratic theory, the history of democratic thought in the African National Congress, participatory democracy in local government, the dominant party system in South Africa, and state–civil society relations.

1

Introduction: Understanding party adaptation

Anthony Butler

After two decades as the party of national government in South Africa, the African National Congress (ANC) is facing unprecedented political challenges. The national and provincial elections in May 2014 demonstrated the vulnerability of the liberation movement to defeat in the most populous and economically pivotal province, Gauteng. It has become clear that the organisational weaknesses of the ANC extend from its candidate selection and leadership election processes, to its membership systems, communications, and money-fuelled politics. As a party of government, the ANC has found itself unable to advance coherent and credible economic and developmental policies. It remains confused about the appropriate relationship between the state and an avowedly 'revolutionary' liberation movement in a constitutional democracy.[1]

Misleading mental maps

There has been abundant analysis of the multi-dimensional predicament of the ANC, by political commentators, scholars, activists and ANC leaders themselves. Much – perhaps most – of this analysis has marched along two broad, well-trodden and ultimately misleading intellectual pathways.

In most public debate, the country's 'dominant party system' –

in which the ANC has enjoyed overwhelming electoral majorities and dominated the political agenda – is viewed as an abnormal and temporary state of affairs. It is widely believed that this system will one day (perhaps very soon) be superseded. It might be replaced by a 'normal' multi-party democracy, in which there is competition for office between a variety of political parties – here the United Kingdom and the United States are common reference points. On the other hand, the dominant party, when confronted with imminent electoral defeat, might refuse to allow competitive elections to be held, and instead use unconstitutional means to retain its grip on power.

These narratives generate two visions of what the future holds for the ANC. One view is that the ANC's electoral prospects will fade, and a flourishing and competitive multi-party system will emerge. The international academic literature on democratic 'transition' has explored this possibility exhaustively in recent years and also examined potential threats to the consolidation of liberal democracy in the country.

The idea that South Africa's political system will 'normalise' into something like a West European multi-party democracy may, however, be deeply misleading. One political scientist recently described the transformation of a dominant party system into a competitive multiparty democracy as akin to 'the passage from adolescence into adulthood' or as a process of 'evolution' and 'maturity'.[2] It is true that longstanding dominant parties in the Global North – including governing parties in Sweden, Canada, Eire and Italy – no longer enjoy electoral dominance or hold ideological sway over their societies. But dominant party systems sometimes take decades to become multi-party systems, and there can be numerous reversals along the way. (We should remark at this point that Japan's Liberal Democratic Party screamed back to power in 2012 just as its demise was once again confidently predicted.) New dominant parties can also emerge where they did not exist before. Meanwhile, the alleged end point of such normalisation processes – the multi-party competitive system – is itself changing in poorly understood ways, and increasingly lacks the competitive and democratic character that has made it hitherto so politically attractive.[3]

The second view of what the future holds is that the liberation movement is destined to become increasingly authoritarian as electoral challenges mount. Some critics have focused on the alleged 'Zanufication' of the ANC. This analysis forms part of a wider set of suppositions about why South Africa will inevitably follow a similar political trajectory to its northern neighbour, Zimbabwe. Some scholars have inadvertently bolstered this conventional wisdom by confining their comparative analysis to African political parties and systems or to national liberation movements in southern Africa.

Events in Zimbabwe over the past decade have certainly provided a riveting spectacle for local elites to watch. And scholars are right to suggest that the comparative study of southern African liberation movements in power can indeed yield significant insights into the trajectory of the ANC.[4] The hopes that were placed in national liberation movements by outside observers and citizens were largely dashed: these movements became authoritarian, intolerant of opposition, deeply corrupt and economically imprudent.[5] In a powerful recent comparative analysis, Roger Southall suggests that they have privileged their own authority over that of the people they claim to represent.[6] They have denigrated their competitors as illegitimate, and advanced patriotic histories of their societies that render opposition politics illegitimate.

These movements share certain historical contexts. Across most of sub-Saharan Africa, colonial powers withdrew rather than being ejected. Where, however, there were significant settler populations that would not concede power, for example in Namibia and Zimbabwe, anti-colonial forces had to engage in armed struggle. This resulted in a change in the character of those movements: they became militaristic, advanced heroic conceptions of their own supposedly revolutionary actions, and developed habits of hierarchy and secrecy that were carried over into the period of liberation. Moreover, the southern African settler societies were economically more advanced than other African states, and they were riven by correspondingly more complex class structures. They depended on extended relationships with international partners, who introduced social democratic, communist, and pan-Africanist ideas into their political doctrines. Southall notes that repeated electoral majorities for these movements, combined with their control of their nations' political agendas, resulted in the blurring of boundaries between state and party. Meanwhile, post-colonial nationalist elites all 'stepped into the shoes' of the departing colonial elites, adopting their lifestyles and pretensions, while cynically transferring resources to themselves under the guise of projects of Africanisation or indigenisation.

However, as Southall himself observes, it is unclear to what extent the ANC's experience as a national liberation movement predisposes it to replicate such political pathologies. Patterns of white domination varied between southern African societies and so generated responses that were quite different in each case. 'The ANC', he notes, 'emerged from struggles within a far more advanced, more complicated, more urbanised, and more diverse society, and its predisposition to embrace difference was a vital outcome.'[7] The settler population is also far bigger in South Africa than in neighbouring countries and it is less able to emigrate. In the economy, the private sector is massively more developed than in neighbouring countries, and it possesses a greater ability to fund redistribution and to accommodate the rent-seeking ambitions of incoming political elites. As a result of such contextual differences, according to Southall, national liberation movements' struggles will have outcomes marked as much 'by their differences as their similarities'.[8]

Thinking comparatively about dominant parties

This book deliberately takes a different approach to the possibilities presented by cross-country comparison in order to bring fresh perspectives to the tired debate about the future of South Africa's party system. The central concept in this analysis is the familiar idea of the 'dominant party system'.[9] On most accounts, the ANC is a classic dominant party, because it has secured resounding national election victories for two decades, it seems set to continue as the party of national government for years to come, and it has dominated the ideological and policy-making landscape of its society.

This field of study pertaining to dominant party systems has produced a number of theoretical and conceptual innovations in recent years, and there is now a rich empirical literature on their rise and fall.[10] Our argument in this book is that there is a special subset of dominant parties that can provide unique insights into the prospects of the ANC. Unlike dominant parties from the most advanced industrialised societies, such as Japan and Italy, these parties conduct politics in middle-income countries at similar levels of development to South Africa. For this reason, they are obliged to negotiate the same kinds of political challenges – inequality, rapid urbanisation, violence, fast-changing class structure – that dog the ANC in South Africa.

Socio-economic and developmental factors, on this analysis, are crucial for framing relevant comparisons. South Africa is a relatively advanced and urbanised economy with a long history of proletarianisation, complex state–business relations, a large middle class, and powerful trade unions. The country's unique history, in the context of sub-Saharan Africa, introduces compelling reasons to compare its political development with that of other middle-income developing countries.

Of the dominant parties in the Global South (or the former 'Third World') an especially important subset, for our purposes, is those parties that have endured electoral defeat (an end to their dominance) or faced a serious prospect of such a defeat. Such parties, explored in this book, include Mexico's Institutional Revolutionary Party (PRI), Taiwan's Kuomintang (KMT), and Malaysia's United Malays National Organisation (UMNO). The Indian National Congress (INC), which emerged in a less developed economy and society, is also included in this study. As we will see, such political parties are not unitary and coherent actors, but they are actors nevertheless; they can adapt in response to defeat or the threat of it, and they are capable not just of surviving in competitive party systems but of thriving in them.

Although the defeat of a dominant party is often heralded as a breakthrough to a new and more democratic era, and as the end of an era of unhealthy political monopoly, such a defeat does not in fact usually result in the disappearance of the former hegemon. There is a common assumption that dominant parties that lose will quickly collapse – and this assumption has shaped the political imagination of many members of South Africa's major opposition party, the Democratic Alliance (DA). They believe that after a breakthrough election in which the ANC stranglehold over the electorate is broken, the hegemon will crumble as its powers of patronage dissipate. It will be broken apart by rival factions, massive defections to opposition parties will begin, and panic, backbiting and recrimination will dominate intra-party politics. The spell that the ANC has, in their view, held over voters will be broken, and the party's history of false promises will finally catch up with it.

In reality, dominant parties rarely fall apart in this way. 'With few exceptions', as Friedman and Wong note in their wide-ranging survey of the trajectories of such organisations, 'most of the former dominant parties survived their defeats.'[11] In the cases of Mexico's PRI and Taiwan's KMT, as we shall see, it proved possible for leaders to lose executive power and then to regain it once again. It is also possible for a dominant party that identifies the danger of defeat before it arrives to take decisive action to defer that unwelcome eventuality.

Party adaptation

Dominant parties in middle-income countries – like any other political party in any kind of party system – can adapt to defeat or to the prospect of it. How and why do they do so? And what lessons can (and will) ANC leaders learn from the successes and failures of other dominant parties?

At first sight, the obstacles to party adaptation are immense. After all, political parties are large organisations, and sociological theory tells us that large organisations are always hard to change. Parties' foundational values and objectives infuse every aspect of the organisation's membership and systems. Party elites are often tied into intricate regional or ideological power balances that have evolved over decades. Wider party organisations are locked into deep-seated relationships with key political constituencies, which cannot be easily broken. Existing constituents, moreover, almost always present obstacles to reaching out to new electorates and support bases. In addition, party bureaucracies refuse to give up power. And political activists, whose lives often revolve around the meaning of the struggle of their chosen party, refuse to concede the need for pragmatic change.

Dominant parties have a history of control and manipulation: this makes their leaders poorly attuned to the demands of survival. Such leaders are also often deeply arrogant and cannot conceive of the possibility of defeat until it is upon them. Sometimes they are rendered blind by ideology. As long-established organisations, dominant parties are also usually deeply 'institutionalised': they have well-developed internal systems, and they have a high degree of autonomy from their environments. Such institutionalisation – viewed in normal times as a marker of party strength and robustness – is, by contrast, an obstacle in times of political adaptation.

The authors in this volume use a variety of theories of party change and adaptation to explain why parties adapt, and to isolate the kinds of adaptation available to party leaders who find themselves confronted by the threat of defeat. Such leaders can change their party's ideology or platform; they can assert fresh values or goals; they can change public policies; they can modify a party's constitution or internal rules, for example concerning candidate selection processes or leadership elections; they can campaign in new ways; or they can enhance or reduce internal party democracy. They can also introduce organisational reforms to improve the functioning of membership systems.

On the other hand, they can also refuse to accept the outcome of legitimate elections, manipulate electoral commissions, change party funding rules, abuse their power over the media, and clamp down on the opposition. Given that complex parties can adapt in so many different ways, and that all of these adaptive efforts have consequences that cannot be reliably predicted, the politics of adaptation are almost always conflict-ridden.

When one is faced with the prospect or reality of defeat, doing nothing is rarely a viable response. But how can we predict when parties will change and in what ways? Beyond deeply informed analysis of how particular parties operate, we can make use of general theories of party dynamics. The most influential theory of party adaptation in the past two decades has been Harmel and Janda's integrated theory of party change.[12] These two scholars concede that party organisations are not easily modified. But they argue that key stimuli, acting independently or together, quite reliably precipitate change in political parties. Electoral defeat, for them, is the most important single factor precipitating party reform. But new leaders, and shifts in the dominant faction or factions of a party, can also bring about change.

Analysing party change is complex. Changes in leadership, factions and electoral performance can all happen simultaneously, and their causal effects can be difficult to disentangle. Harmel and Janda's key insight is that adaptation must be understood in the light of the goals of a party. Poor electoral performance, for example, will not prove to be a major shock for a party that is seeking influence rather than office. A party expecting a landslide win may be shocked even in victory, if that win is unexpectedly narrow. Policy-oriented parties can be shaken up by changes in the relevance or credibility of their programmes.

The goals of parties, of course, are themselves rarely clear. Most parties incorporate a mix of vote-seeking, office-seeking and policy-oriented behaviours. Sections of the party in government, in parliament, in party organisations and in the country may understand the objectives of their party in distinct ways. Nevertheless, theories of party change can provide a useful intellectual tool for understanding how parties adapt.

In this book we also explore two potential sources of deliberate political and organisational learning for the ANC: the Brazilian Workers' Party (Partido dos Trabalhadores, or PT) and the Communist Party of China (CPC). Brazil and China are now ostensibly pivotal partners as a result of a new South–South diplomacy that has brought about South African participation in the BRICS (Brazil, Russia, India, China, South Africa) grouping of emerging economies. The Congress of South

African Trade Unions has championed Brazil's purported 'Lula moment' as a culmination of trade union influence in the PT and public policy innovation oriented towards alleviating poverty and inequality. While the CPC dominates a quite different and authoritarian political system, it has also been advanced as a role model by influential ANC leaders.

Country cases

Let us sum up the approach of this book. Our contributors use general theories of party change from political science that explain why, and in what ways, political parties adapt. Rather than looking at African comparators, contributors explore political parties in middle-income developing countries in the Global South that share many of South Africa's socio-economic and socio-political characteristics. The key country cases investigate how dominant parties that have been in power for decades respond to electoral defeat or the prospect of it. Finally, some contributors also look at prominent political parties from which ANC strategists have deliberately tried to learn in recent years.

In Chapter 2, the first of our case studies, Alexander Tan explores the organisational learning of the Kuomintang in democratic Taiwan. The KMT, a mainland Chinese party exiled to Taiwan after losing the civil war, was an authoritarian ruling party until the late 1970s when a slow political liberalisation began. After unexpected defeats in the 2000 and 2004 presidential elections, the party introduced a range of reforms that allowed it to recapture the presidency in 2008. As Tan shows, the electoral shocks were a wake-up call to the party elite, and resulted in changes to the party leadership; to campaigning, candidate selection, gender and organisational systems; to party finance and corporate assets; and to the ability of criminals and corrupt politicians to survive in the party. However, the KMT continues to be a centralised party with limited opportunities for participation by members. And reforms have slowed or even reversed now that the party is firmly back in power. Defeat may be the mother of all change, as Tan suggests; but resurrection has proved to be a great dampener of reformist zeal.

The second case study, in Chapter 3, explores the defeat, and return to power, of Mexico's Institutional Revolutionary Party (PRI). PRI held power for longer than any other non-communist party in history, taking control of Mexico's federal government in 1929 and holding the presidency until 2000. As Kenneth Greene has shown elsewhere,[13] the party's incumbency advantages – especially a politicisation of public resources – allowed it to buy votes and dominate elections without resort to massive fraud.

The PRI lost power when economic crisis robbed it of its ability to skew elections in its favour. In order to survive, Kenneth Greene and Hector Ibarra-Rueda explain, PRI had to change, but party leaders were not well placed to adapt. Conflict between the national and state-level party organisations ultimately changed the balance of power in the PRI, and (somewhat fortuitously) the party was saved by a 'strategy of federalism'.

Factionalism and disunity were crucial factors at provincial level. Provinces with 'accommodative factionalism' were able to campaign effectively. Those experiencing 'conflictual factionalism', by contrast, were preoccupied with debilitating internal battles and could not campaign successfully. PRI is thriving in a competitive party system in part because of a successful accommodation between the relative powers of the centre and the regions. As Greene and Ibarra-Rueda show, party adaptation can depend on the negotiation of an appropriate balance between central authority and provincial decentralisation.

In Chapter 4, Edmund Terence Gomez explores the enduring power of the United Malays National Organisation (UMNO) in Malaysian politics. Despite eroding electoral support, especially among the urban middle classes, the party has successfully used racialised discourses, media manipulation, party funding abuses and patronage politics to retain office, most recently in a hard-fought election in May 2013. Malaysian politics share many features with those of South Africa. Affirmative action policies designed to advance the interests of the Malay majority have spawned a vast patronage system that has fuelled factional division in UMNO. At the same time, factional entities are pacified by the distribution of state rents. Gomez suggests that the society is rapidly changing – most notably its class structure and urbanisation – and that UMNO will soon prove unable to adapt to such change.

Chapter 5 turns to the Partido dos Trabalhadores (PT) – the Workers' Party of Brazil. PT has been praised by elements in the ANC tripartite alliance for innovations in public policy that have starkly reduced economic inequality and poverty. Guilherme Reis contends, however, that the positive impact of having a party of the left in power has increasingly been neutralised by changes in the factional politics of the party. PT avowedly pursues substantive goals such as reducing inequality and poverty and advancing the interests of ordinary workers. But, under pressure of electoral competition, it has become dominated by electoralist factions that have as their primary goal the winning of presidential elections. Changes in the party are partly explained by its 'front' character: it was built out of many diverse groups that opposed military rule. As the party has developed a more oligarchic and professionalised structure, and 'moderate' factions have taken over its leadership and bureaucracy, it has abandoned many of the ideological and political factors that lie behind its much-vaunted successes.

Chapter 6 turns to the Chinese Communist Party (CPC) and explores one fascinating aspect of that party's mechanics of social control. The CPC operates in a very different political and socio-economic context from that of the other parties in this volume. The relationship between the ruling party and the state is conceptualised in China as steeply hierarchical, although there are continuous coded deliberations within the party elite about the desirability of some form of constitutional government. In recent years the ANC has established close relationships with the CPC, and there has been an ostensible process of learning from and emulation of what are taken to be CPC's attractive features. Modernisation without westernisation has proved an attractive idea for many ANC leaders. As Martyn Davies has observed,[14] the 'Chinese model' has had a significant impact on ANC conceptions of desirable economic and political change. A programme has been instituted in which members of the ANC's National Executive Committee visit the Beijing party school to understand the character of the party-state and the alleged benefits of state-directed development and preferential state financing.

In their chapter, Ping Shum and Zheng Yongnian explore the CPC's use of information and communications technologies to manage the party-state and build popular legitimacy. The rise of the Internet and mobile telecommunications poses threats to authoritarian regimes but also presents opportunities. The CPC has used new technologies to shape public opinion, improve monitoring of cadre performance, and combat low-level corruption while bolstering central control by the party.

In Chapter 7, Thiven Reddy uses a comparative analysis of factional politics in the Indian National Congress (INC) and the ANC to explore the political disintegration of dominant parties. Writing in the aftermath of the decimation of the INC in India's 2014 elections, he observes that its organisational weaknesses developed across decades. His analysis, echoing that of Greene and others in this volume, indicates that some kinds of factionalism are inimical to the unity that dominant parties need to survive. But the 'cooperative factionalism' that liberation movements such as the INC initially enjoy turns over time into a 'competitive factionalism' that requires active and skilled management by party elites. As factions embed themselves in the party's own organisational systems, and reproduce themselves in contests for party positions, the focus of political life shifts inexorably from contests with other parties to internal battles for position. Ultimately a degenerative factionalism is likely to set in that can tear a party apart.

In Chapter 8, Vinothan Naidoo develops a related aspect of dominant parties' success and failure: their ability to manage relationships between state and party over long periods in government. Naidoo explores the ANC's practice of 'deployment' of party cadres to state and parastatal positions, setting out its relationship to patronage, clientelism and the project of racial transformation. Deployment creates parallel systems of accountability and is likely to be hijacked by different sites of power in a party; it can therefore become an expression of factionalism rather than a mechanism to contain it. Naidoo ends with an investigation of ANC responses to abuses of deployment such as 'careerism' (the use of party office for private gain). He is somewhat sceptical about the potential merit of political education and the monitoring of cadre performance.

In the final chapter, Heidi Brooks Yung investigates the ANC's own recent discussion documents on organisational renewal. The ANC has set out quite trenchant critiques of its own performance, citing the so-called 'sins of incumbency' that bedevil a party of power, the perils of proximity to state resources, challenges to the internal stability of the movement, and the growth of competitive factionalism. The movement has also drawn up plans to address more narrowly organisational weaknesses in the ANC's candidate selection processes, membership systems and neglect of information technologies. Yung's analysis suggests that the ANC does not know how to realise its ambition to be the strategic 'centre of power' in the society, and that its proposals for political education, the creation of a 'new cadre' and the management of civil society activism are instrumental and potentially anti-democratic.

I will return in the conclusion to explore some of the implications of these analyses for our understanding of the possible futures of the ANC.

2

The organisational learning of the Kuomintang in democratic Taiwan

Alexander Tan

In 2000 the Kuomintang (Chinese Nationalist Party or KMT) was voted out of executive power in Taiwan. In a political system that is dominated by the executive branch, the KMT was unprepared for being in the opposition and found itself in the uncharacteristic position of being without access to the usual resources when it had controlled and dominated Taiwan's politics. In view of the shock of being kicked out of office and the spectre of having to stay out of power, party change was initiated, though not without problems and internal conflict. Already, there are signs that the transformation of the KMT into an electoral-professional' party[1] or an 'election machine' has stalled.[2] Furthermore, as Taiwan's democracy is consolidated and further deepens, the dynamics of an electoral democracy and Taiwan's constitutional arrangements are leading to a redefinition of the proper association between the KMT and the state (whether the party is in or out of government) as well as of the proper relationship between the parliamentary and the extra-parliamentary wings of the party.

Using the literature on party change for theoretical guidance, in this chapter I examine the organisational learning of the KMT that led to its reform and modernisation. In the first section, I conduct a very brief review of the party change literature, focusing on the factors that have been identified as stimuli to organisational change. After this discussion,

I provide the background to Taiwan's KMT, after which I examine the transformation of the party since Taiwan's political liberalisation, which began in 1986 and saw a democratic transition taking place in earnest in 1996. In the last section, I re-examine how the theories of party change can help us understand the changes (or lack of them) within the KMT.

Why do parties change?

As with most large organisations, political parties are conservative organisations that are reluctant to change. Why, then, do they? In their pioneering and seminal work of 1994, Harmel and Janda proposed an integrated theory of party change, suggesting that it results from changes in leadership, in the dominant faction or coalition, and in environmental stimuli, or a combination of these factors.[3] The literature on party change is rich with empirical studies that have corroborated many of the theoretical propositions from Harmel and Janda's work.

As an extension of their theoretical framework, I examined in a work published in 2002 the transformation of the Kuomintang immediately after its shock defeat in the 2000 presidential election.[4] I derived three hypotheses from Harmel and Janda's integrated theory of party change and empirically tested them using the KMT's development until late 2000 as evidence. Specifically, the three hypotheses can be summarised as follows: (1) poor electoral performance will lead to party change; (2) leadership change will lead to party change; and (3) changes in the dominant faction will lead to party change. Let me very briefly explain these three hypotheses.

The first hypothesis, as we have seen, posits that poor electoral performance will bring about party change. As large organisations, political parties can be conservative in terms of initiating internal organisational transformation. This stems from the fact that parties are constrained by their ideologies and social support base, as well as by the fact that they are platforms that serve to hold together delicate power balances among like-minded political elites. Being in a state of delicate equilibrium, 'parties tend to resist change' and changes are not undertaken lightly for fear of upsetting the status quo.[5] Yet changes in parties do occur. According to Janda, a party's poor electoral performance is a strong stimulus for transformation: 'defeat is the mother of all change'.[6]

However, to attribute all party change simply to poor electoral performance neglects the role that party actors play within the organisation. Besides poor electoral performance, the impact of party leaders, activists and members is also an important reason why party change occurs. In particular, the role of leadership cannot be neglected.[7] The second hypothesis states that leadership change leads to party change. In their attempt to consolidate their power in the party or to simply leave a mark or a legacy, new leaders (or any leader for that matter) normally propose, initiate and implement changes during their tenure. As a scholar of complex organisation notes, 'leadership transitions represent a natural entry point for change … Leadership transitions are … volatile moments in the life cycles of organizations, occasions for renewal as well as for regression.'[8] A historical example of party change resulting from leadership change was noted by Robert Michels in his classic study of the German Social Democratic Party (SPD), who showed episodes of leadership change followed by occasions of organisational change.[9] Harmel, Janda, Heo and Tan have shown that even after credit is given for the impact of electoral performance on party change, leadership change continues to be a significant exogenous factor accounting for changes within the party organisation.[10]

Lastly, despite the fact that political parties are made up of actors who may share similar ideology and may have relatively similar views on the proper role of the state and the relationship between state and citizens, these same actors can still take up different positions on issues relating to the party's identity, strategy, leadership or goals. As a result, when a faction or coalition wrests control of the party leadership from another, it is likely that party change will occur.[11] In a later work, Harmel and Tan have refined this hypothesis, taking account of the intensity of factional rivalry, the completeness and comprehensiveness of the factional or coalitional replacement, as well as the co-occurrence of party leadership change.[12]

These three hypotheses have largely found support in the history of Taiwan's KMT until 2001. Since 2001 the KMT has endured other electoral setbacks in subsequent presidential and legislative elections as well as weathering party splits. In 2008 the KMT won the presidency and since then has dominated the legislature. Throughout the period 2000–13, the KMT initiated numerous programmes that proposed changes to the party organisation. Some have been successfully implemented while the progress of others has been noticeably slower.

The Kuomintang and Taiwan's political context

Established as a revolutionary organisation during the latter years of the Manchu dynasty in China, the KMT was exiled to Taiwan in 1949 after losing a protracted civil war – interrupted by the Second World War – to the Chinese Communist Party (CCP). Organised as a Leninist party, the KMT firmly established control of all aspects of political life in Taiwan.[13] From 1949 to 1975, the KMT can be aptly described as restrictive, hierarchical and authoritarian. During this period, the KMT was a party dominated primarily by Chinese (or their descendants) who came to Taiwan after 1947 – the so-called mainlanders, in Taiwan's political vocabulary. After Chiang Kai-shek's death in 1975, the mantle passed to his son, Chiang Ching-kuo.

In the early years of Chiang Ching-kuo's stewardship, the party did not change its character and organisation substantially. Its key decision-making positions continued to be dominated by mainlanders. Organisationally, the KMT continued to maintain a Leninist mass party structure, with a Central Committee and a Central Standing Committee acting as an advisory council to the party chairman. As the charisma of the party chairman dominated the critical affairs of the party, intraparty democracy was absent. Selection for membership of the two most powerful committees – the Central Committee and Central Standing Committee – was by appointment by the party chairman. The Central Standing Committee appointed legislative candidates, with the party chairman playing an important veto role. Furthermore, the selection of the party chairman was made simply by confirmation of the National

Congress rather than by voting.

When the United States ended formal diplomatic relations with Taiwan in 1979, the KMT began to change and readjust its role in Taiwan. As it realised that unification with China was no longer tenable as a party policy position, the party began shifting its focus to the affairs of the island of Taiwan. It slowly opened itself to recruiting islanders into leadership roles. From 1979 to 1986, though the organisation and structure of the KMT did not change substantially, this period under the party chairmanship of Chiang Ching-kuo[14] saw the gradual redefinition of the KMT as a Taiwanese party, rather than a Chinese party occupying Taiwan temporarily.

The creation of the Democratic Progressive Party – Taiwan's first legal, organised opposition – in 1986 and the death of Chiang Ching-kuo two years later led to an acceleration of the movement towards political liberalisation and the culmination of the democratic transition in Taiwan. The KMT inaugurated a new era when electing its first islander party chairman, Lee Teng-hui, who by virtue of being state vice-president assumed the presidency after the death of Chiang Ching-kuo. Under the chairmanship of Lee Teng-hui, the KMT witnessed significant changes whose reverberations continue to affect the KMT and Taiwanese politics today. From being a hegemonic party when Lee took control in 1988, the KMT lost the presidential election in 2000 and was relegated to an unaccustomed role as an opposition party. Resigning to take responsibility for the electoral defeat, Lee was replaced by another islander, Lien Chan, who initiated numerous reforms in order to bring the party back to power.[15] After another defeat in 2004, the party was thrown into soul-searching exercises and began a series of reforms to ensure its return to power. In 2005 Lien Chan was replaced by Ma Ying-jeou, who helped reposition the party so as to capture the presidency in 2008 and then win a successful re-election in 2012 for a second term as state president. At the same time, the KMT was able to regain lost ground in legislative elections in 2008 and then held on to its majority status in 2012.

In Taiwan, the ideological divide among the major parties has less on a left–right dimension, as in other industrial democracies; nor do parties align along rural–urban or liberal–conservative dimensions, as in many developing countries. Given the unique situation of the country and its relation to China, Taiwan's political parties are arrayed along the national identity dimension. Essentially, this potent cleavage reflects Taiwan's political and international status in relation to China: the one side holds the view that Taiwan is part of a greater China with which it will eventually be unified, while the other side holds that Taiwan is not part of a greater China and is a completely separate nation-state.

In reality, Taiwan's parties form two broad camps: the pan-Blue alliance and the pan-Green alliance. Each alliance is named after the colour of the flag of the largest party in the camp. The pan-Blue alliance, which is led by the KMT and includes its splinter parties – People's First Party (PFP) and New Party (NP), claims that Taiwan, though currently a separate territory, is part of a larger mainland China. While reunification with the People's Republic is not its immediate aim, the pan-Blue alliance is based on a very strong Chinese national identity. The pan-Green alliance, led by the Democratic Progressive Party (DPP) and the Taiwan Solidarity Union (TSU), has a very strong islander identity and calls for Taiwan's de jure independence.[16]

In terms of the political system, vestiges of the exiled Republic of China government still exist in Taiwan today, such as the state constitution, which was brought over from China but has over time been revised to fit Taiwan's circumstances. Taiwan currently has a semi-presidential system of government, with some unique features that differentiate it from the French system. The president, who is head of the executive yuan (branch), is popularly elected for a four-year term, with a two-term limit.[17] The president, who is independent of the legislative yuan (Taiwan's parliament), appoints the premier, who heads the cabinet. The premier and the cabinet serve at the pleasure of the president although they are also responsible to the legislative yuan. In Taiwan's semi-presidentialism, the premier and cabinet are not members of the legislature, nor is the president obligated to appoint the leader of the majority party or coalition to lead the cabinet. The legislature can call for a no-confidence vote, forcing a change in cabinet and premier, but the president can in turn dissolve the legislature and call for new elections. This Taiwanese version of semi-presidentialism creates its own unique set of incentives and disincentives for political actors in the political system, which has particular implications for reform within the KMT.

Furthermore, beginning in 2008, Taiwan's electoral system changed from a single non-transferable vote (SNTV) system with multiple seat constituencies to a mixed member majoritarian (MMM) system giving voters two ballots – one for a constituency seat and another for a party. At the same time that the new electoral system was implemented, Taiwan reduced the size of its parliamentary seats from 225 to 113, of which 73 are constituency seats, six aboriginal seats, and 34 seats allocated to party lists. As with the constitutional structures and arrangements, the electoral system creates unique dynamics for party reform, at least within the KMT – a point we will revisit later.

Electoral performance and transformation of the KMT

Since the transition to democracy, the KMT's electoral performance has experienced some ups and downs. Table 1 shows the electoral support in presidential elections since the first direct election of the president in 1996, while Table 2 shows the percentage of legislative seats held by the KMT.

In Table 1, we can see the calamitous election result of 2000 for the KMT, which led to Taiwan's first turnover of executive government to the opposition. In the 2000 presidential election, the KMT suffered a split in its ranks when the former KMT secretary-general James Soong stood as an independent candidate and split the KMT (and pan-Blue) vote to allow Chen Shui-bian of the DPP to capture the presidency. As if to add insult to injury, the KMT lost its majority in the 2002–5 legislative yuan (see Table 2) for the first time in its history. The KMT was only able to hold onto control of the legislature by forming a coalition with its pan-Blue allies. In 2004 the pan-Blue alliance coalesced around the KMT party chairman, Lien Chan, and bitterly contested the

Table 1: KMT's performance in presidential elections, 1996–2012

Year	%
1996	54%
2000	23.1%
2004	49.89%
2008	58.45%
2012	51.6%

Source: Central Election Commission

Table 2: KMT's share of the legislative yuan, 1998–2012

Year	%
1998	54.67%
2002	30.22%
2005	35.11%
2008	71.68%
2012	56.64%

Source: Central Election Commission

presidential election, only to lose by the closest of margin (0.22 per cent) to the incumbent President Chen.[18] This was then followed by a poor electoral performance for the legislature, such that the KMT failed to gain a plurality of seats in the 2005–8 legislature and again needed to rely on its allies to achieve a legislative majority.

It was not until the legislative elections in January 2008 and the presidential election in March 2008 that the KMT captured both the legislature and the presidency again. Riding on the popularity of 'Mr Clean' – Ma Ying-jeou – and benefiting from the corruption scandals surrounding the incumbent President Chen, the KMT won a supermajority in the legislature and then a strong majority in the presidential election, enabling it to wrest the presidency and executive branch back. Though in the 2012 election the KMT lost votes and seats, it was still able to hold onto control of both the executive and legislative branches.

It is without doubt that the poor electoral performance of the KMT has been a stimulus for party reform and change. True to Janda's theory, 'poor electoral performance is the mother of change' in the KMT.[19] Using its electoral performance as a backdrop, we can examine the reforms of the KMT by classifying them according to different periods following its shock loss of the presidency in 2000.[20]

From hegemon to opposition, 2000 to 2008

The electoral shocks of both the 2000 presidential election and the December 2001 legislative election administered a wake-up call for the KMT. Unaccustomed to being an opposition party, the KMT had to scramble to redefine its relationship with the state almost immediately after the 2000 presidential election. The party chairman, Lee Teng-hui, resigned his post and gave way to Lien Chan, who immediately sought to reform the KMT by establishing a party affairs reform committee (PARC) to 'streamline the party by making it a young, localized, pluralistic, grassroots, volunteer-based democratic party'[21] and reforming it to become electorally successful or an 'election machine'.[22] Significant changes were also made to allow for the direct election of the party chairman, the use of primary elections for legislative candidate selection, the creation of quotas for women and minorities, placement of party businesses in blind trusts, and dismissal of party members with criminal records.[23]

Additionally, the KMT undertook an organisational restructuring to streamline its substantial bureaucratic structure, though Chen argues that its fundamental characteristics and attributes as a party leading the state (as a revolutionary party) has not altered or been compromised.[24] Chen notes that one significant change was made to the composition of the top decision-making body – the Central Standing Committee (CSC).[25] Prior to 2000, the CSC was dominated by party members who also held cabinet or government positions. However, since the KMT's loss of the presidency in 2000, the CSC has become more influenced by the parliamentary party. Other organisational changes include removing layers of party bureaucracy from district to national level and reducing the number of party personnel.

The calls to transform the KMT into an election machine became louder and more pronounced following the loss of its legislative majority in the December 2001 elections. Yet, despite these calls the KMT has not made much progress in undertaking reforms to become an electoral-professional party. It continues to be a highly bureaucratic party and party decision-making remains centralised.[26]

The KMT's poor electoral showing continued after 2001. In early 2004 the party lost a bitterly contested presidential election. Nonetheless, it did not undertake further significant internal changes nor made concerted efforts to examine the reasons for its electoral defeat in what Fell termed a 'wasted year'.[27] In the December 2004 election, the party still failed to gain a plurality of votes, which led to a change in the party chairmanship in 2005, with party members electing Ma Ying-jeou.[28] As the party remained 'out-of-government', it continued to attempt to reform itself as an election machine by burnishing its image as a 'clean' and 'visionary' party.[29] Changes were made to the Central Standing Committee, increasing the membership from 31 to 32 and including the Young KMT leader as an ex-officio member. One of the most notable developments in the period 2000–8 has been the growing clout of the parliamentary wing of the party vis-à-vis the extra-parliamentary wing.

Back to power and forward to the past, 2008 to the present

In 2008 the KMT was swept back to power in both the legislative and the presidential elections. Interestingly, in 2008 and 2009, President Ma did not concurrently hold the position of KMT party chairman, unlike earlier KMT leaders. It was at this juncture that the increasing tensions between the parliamentary wing, the extra-parliamentary wing and the party-in-government became obvious. With President Ma taking a back seat and allowing cabinet government to operate, the increasing independence of KMT legislators has made policy coordination very difficult, as evidenced by the low success rates of government-sponsored bills.[30]

Because of the difficulties of policy coordination between the two wings of the party, the KMT vigorously debated the issue of the concurrent holding of the party chairmanship by the state president.

If the party is to transform itself to be more like political parties in presidential systems, such as that of the United States, it is not necessary for the president to be also the party chairman. However, as the essence and character of the KMT derives from concept of the 'party guiding the state (or the government)', and given that the nature of Taiwan's version of semi-presidentialism has created incentives for the KMT to maintain the status quo, the party chairmanship and the state presidency are still held by the same person.

President Ma decided to stand for the position of party chairman and in July 2009 won the election. He then appointed King Pu-tsung to serve as party secretary-general from 2009 to 2011. During this period, the relationship between the party-in-government, the extra-parliamentary wing and the parliamentary wing has been recalibrated. A priority has been the reform of the party's corporate assets and the call for the acceleration of the move towards an electoral-professional party became more prominent. The party also became a platform for policy coordination at a national level by creating various ad hoc groups and permanent committees to allow the top leaders in government, the legislature and the party to meet regularly.

Interestingly, despite secretary-general King Pu-tsung's call to turn the KMT into an electoral-professional party, the party continues to be quite vague in its own understanding of what this would mean other than being successful in election campaigns and winning elections.[31] Today, the KMT is streamlined and relatively leaner with fewer paid party bureaucrats, but it still remains a large bureaucratic organisation. There are slightly more opportunities for party members to participate and at some levels the party is more internally democratic when compared with what it was pre-2004 and certainly prior to 2000. But it is nowhere near becoming an electoral-professional party nor is power more decentralised in the party itself. In fact, it continues to be a mass-bureaucratic organisation and, after its return to power in 2008, there has been significantly more centralisation of power as the president has extended his control of the party organisation. Given the low popularity of President Ma's administration in his 'lame-duck' term that began with his re-election in early 2012, intra-party realignments and factional rivalries are coming to the fore. The re-election contest for the party chairmanship in late 2012 and the very public jostling for power between the speaker of the legislature (who is a very senior and experienced KMT member) and President Ma are just two examples of intra-party conflicts and realignments. KMT reforms since 2008 have been slow and perfunctory rather than significant and meaningful.[32]

Learning to lose or hard habits to break?
No political party organises itself to lose an election. When the KMT lost the presidential election in 2000, it found itself in the unfamiliar situation of not having control of the executive branch, from where its tentacles reached a long way into Taiwanese society. It then kickstarted a process of internal party reform in the hope that it would bring the party back to power again. Yet, it is important to note here that despite losing control of the executive branch, the KMT kept its hold on the legislature all throughout the period it was in 'opposition', thereby creating a divided government in Taiwan. This episode of divided government during 2000–8 – where the DPP held the executive branch and the KMT the legislative – was fraught and characterised by executive–legislative conflict and inefficiencies. We also need to be reminded that, unlike other political parties, the KMT commands huge corporate resources, an intensive and extensive organisational structure, and a significant electoral support base. In many ways, these factors also serve as stumbling blocks to continued democratic reform of the KMT. The stumbling blocks are both external and internal in kind. Among the external factors we can include Taiwan's constitutional structure as well as the electoral system itself, while internal factors include factional and leadership competition as well as the party's own perception of its electoral performance.

As mentioned earlier, the constitutional structure of Taiwan creates a unique set of incentives and disincentives for party reform and that of the KMT in particular. The semi-presidential system of Taiwan is a half-baked assemblage of features of the French system combined with those of the constitution that was originally developed for China and then revised numerous times to fit the needs of Taiwan. The premier and his cabinet are appointed by the president but are responsible to the legislature. Moreover, the premier and cabinet, contrary to the parliamentary system and even the French system, are not members of the legislature. In this sense, the Taiwanese executive is not a fusion of various systems but a unique power system like that of the United States.[33]

Organised as a Leninist party and in total control of the government and the state bureaucracy, the KMT has always operated in terms of the 'party-state' concept. The permeation of party into the state sees the party directing the state apparatus but also sees the government having the benefit of the party apparatus for effective governance. For the KMT, then, the possibility of separating the party–state relationship becomes a very difficult issue, as it strikes at the very core of its organisational being. In fact, the separation of party and state was forced upon the KMT when it lost control of the executive between 2000 and 2008. During this period in opposition, the parliamentary wing became the party's most prominent face. It was also at this time that the KMT experienced the most thoroughgoing reform. The question of the proper relationship between party and state was raised just as the KMT retreated from control of the executive apparatus of the Taiwanese state.

Yet, after 2008 the party–state issue became prominent again within the party as the KMT faced a more vocal and independent parliamentary wing, a party chairman that has no official government position and a state president not leading the party. Should the state president also be the party chairman? This question, then, goes to the core of the relationship between the parliamentary and extra-parliamentary wings as well as their relationship to the party-in-government. The shift from the SNTV electoral system to the MMM one only served to make this issue more prominent. The use of primaries in legislative candidate selection and the establishment of single-member constituencies created a group of legislators who can be relatively independent of the executive branch. These legislators can cultivate their own local power bases, which may help them to become indispensable to the party and also reduce the ability of the party to enforce party discipline, especially when it comes to supporting government-sponsored bills in the legislature. But if the incumbent state president is outside the party executive and the premier and cabinet are not members of the legislature, party discipline is compromised and substantially weakened, and so is the ability of the government and the president's administration to push important government legislation.

In effect, Taiwan's constitutional structure has created a complex set of three KMTs – the party-in-government, the parliamentary party and the extra-parliamentary party. For the KMT, and an issue for any governing party in Taiwan, this then becomes a problem of coordination, efficiency, and effectiveness between all three parts of the party. In the end, the KMT decided that rather than decentralise the party, it should actually concentrate more power at the top level by creating coordinating mechanisms led by the president or his designated representative, the party secretary-general.

Internal factors that serve as stumbling blocks to continued democratic reform of the party include factional and leadership competition as well its success in recapturing the executive branch. The KMT has several patriarchs with a very loyal following within the party. The incomplete reform of the party observed by Chen can be attributed to disagreement within the dominant coalition on how to proceed with party reforms that would turn the KMT into an electoral-professional party.[34] As Harmel and Tan suggest, 'the ability of a newly dominant faction to fully direct the party rests on whether the change in conformation has resulted (either immediately, or ultimately through a series of discrete changes) in complete rather than just partial turnover of the dominant coalition and also on whether the party's effective leaders are fully committed to the objectives of the newly dominant faction/coalition'.[35]

Lastly, the adage 'if it ain't broke, don't fix it' is appropriate in partly explaining the resistance to more significant reforms in the KMT. Since 2008, the KMT has been able to retain control of both the executive and legislative branches of government. This relative electoral success, despite the poorer showing in 2012, has dampened the zeal and appetite for more substantial intra-party democratic reforms. KMT's recent electoral 'success' has been aided by the electoral system change – from SNTV to MMM – making it difficult for its splinter parties (and pan-Blue allies), like the people's First Party and the New Party, to challenge the KMT for pan-Blue votes. In this way the KMT's powerful position in the Taiwanese party system has been consolidated and it has been given some sense of electoral security.

Conclusion

So why did the KMT initiate party reforms and why has the KMT stalled in carrying out some of its reforms? By using the perspective of theories of party change, the answer to these questions can be summarised in the roles that electoral performance, leadership and factions play in instigating (or stalling) party reform. In this brief exposition of the reforms undertaken by the KMT since 2000, the evidence largely corroborates the importance in generating the impetus for party change, reform and renewal of the dynamics of external factors such as constitutional structures and poor electoral performance and their interaction with internal factors such as leadership and factions.

3

Mexico's Institutional Revolutionary Party: Reform and resurgence

Kenneth F. Greene and Hector Ibarra-Rueda

Transitions from dominant party rule to fully competitive multi-party democracy are heralded events. Victorious opposition candidates typically extol their successes as the triumph of the people's choice over electoral fraud, clean government over corruption, good economic management over bad, and the rise of a new generation over the political manoeuvrings of an older, out-of-touch political class. The winning challenger to Mexico's long-ruling dominant party, the conservative politician Vicente Fox, embodied these characteristics when he likened his struggle for the presidency to Lech Walesa's Solidarity Movement in Poland and to Nelson Mandela's quest for freedom and justice in South Africa.[1]

In the light of the claim that turnover represents transformation, one might expect that formerly dominant parties would quickly disappear. Rather than remaking themselves into viable democratic competitors, they would be torn asunder by rival factions no longer controlled by the country's chief executive and they would die slowly as candidates defect to rising opposition parties. Even if democratic dominant parties in Italy, Japan, Sweden, India and Luxembourg could remain viable in newly competitive systems, surely authoritarian dominant parties in Mexico, Paraguay, Taiwan and Senegal would disappear as voters reject their past record of electoral fraud, fiscal favouritism, widespread patronage and selective repression.²

Yet most dominant parties have successfully transformed into democratic competitors. Formerly dominant parties in Mexico, Taiwan and Paraguay have even won the presidency again. What allows parties to make the transition from dominance to democrats, from controlling the political system to becoming a viable player in a newly competitive regime?

In this chapter, we argue that Mexico's Institutional Revolutionary Party (PRI) survived and thrived because it adopted what we term the 'strategy of federalism'. By delegating authority from national leaders to subnational party units, the PRI's (subnational) state party organisations were better able to respond to voters' demands and either retain or quickly win back powerful governorships during the country's protracted transition to democracy. The party's subnational staying power sustained it after losing the presidency in 2000 and helped it come back to national prominence by becoming the plurality winner in the 2009 midterm elections and returning to the presidential palace in 2012.

Despite the PRI's successful adaptation from dominance to democracy, the process was anything but consensual. Conflicts between national leaders seeking to maintain centralised control and local leaders seeking to decentralise it nearly tore the party apart. The PRI's experience is thus a cautionary tale for other dominant parties facing rising competition, suggesting that the federalist strategy can save such parties but that the transition from the old centralised organisational schema to the newer decentralised one may doom them in the process.

The first section of this chapter describes the PRI's decline and resurgence. The second section contrasts existing arguments about the importance of leaders' autonomy for party adaptation with our own argument that lower-level cadres are the main force for adaptation in dominant parties facing rising competition, whereas national leaders oppose reform. The third section describes two periods of PRI organisation: a long period of hierarchical centralised control under national party leadership during the era of unquestioned single-party dominance that lasted until 1990, and the subsequent period of reform that resulted in a more decentralised organisation with the onset of fully competitive democracy in 2000. The bridge between the old and new organisational equilibriums was marked by fights between national and state party leaders that threatened to doom the party. The final section before the conclusion shows that, ironically, state party organisations that were best able to resist the national party's incursions before democratisation were the best positioned to win governorships and thus help the PRI come back to national prominence. The conclusion draws out lessons about party organisation for dominant parties facing rising competition.

Decline and resurgence of the PRI

The PRI, and its predecessors under different names, held power for longer than any non-communist party in history. It dominated 20th-century politics in Mexico, taking control of the federal government in 1929 with the consolidation of the post-revolutionary political regime, and holding the presidency until 2000. It also held a super-majority in Congress until 1988 and a simple majority until 1997 as well as all state governorships until 1989.

During the period of single-party dominance, elections were minimally free but maximally unfair. Elections occurred at regular, constitutionally mandated intervals and all opposition parties were allowed to compete; however, until the 1990s, the PRI used what Kenneth Greene refers to as its hyper-incumbency advantages to tilt the partisan playing field in its favour and virtually win elections before election day.[3] Three advantages were key. The party used its control over the federal government to 'firefight' threats of dissident social groups by enacting policies that strategically satisfied these groups' demands; it used its control over the purse strings to politicise public resources and dramatically outspend competitors in all aspects of campaigning as well as through vote-buying; and it used selective and episodic repression against challengers that could not be bought.

The PRI lost national-level power in a protracted transition to fully competitive democracy, which started with the 1982 debt crisis and culminated with the opposition winning the presidency in 2000. The economic crisis and subsequent free-market policy response diminished the PRI's ability to generate resource advantages from the public budget. Several rounds of economic privatisations reduced the size of the public pie from which the PRI took liberal slices. The state's declining role in the economy also made potential donors less reliant on the PRI for government largesse. As resource asymmetries between the incumbent party and its challengers declined, the PRI lost vote share, eventually leading to turnover.[4]

One would naturally expect the PRI to lose subnational offices as voters turned against its national-level candidates. Indeed, support for opposition parties began to rise in many states well before the PRI lost the presidency. The conservative National Action Party (PAN) won its first governorship in 1989 and, by the time the PRI lost its majority in Congress in 1997, opposition parties held 22 per cent of the 32 federal entities (31 governorships plus the Federal District). By the time of the historic 2000 elections, when the PRI lost the presidency, the PAN and leftist Party of the Democratic Revolution (PRD) together held 41 per cent of the governorships.

But rather than disappearing as opposition parties swept up subnational elections following its loss of the presidency, the formerly dominant party rebounded in state elections starting in 2002. It stopped the opposition's march by retaining governorships in nine states where it has never lost and by 2013, it had won back 12 more states after sitting out of power for an average of 1.8 terms. In the remaining 11 states, it lost power at some point after 1989 and has not yet returned, but in five of these it has only been out for one term and so may come back.

The PRI's continued success in state-level elections was important for its subsequent comeback at the national level, which began later. Field reports indicate that PRI governors used discretionary resources as well as the bully pulpit to bolster campaigns.[5] In both its 2009 comeback in congressional midterm elections and its successful bid for the presidency in 2012, the states where it had previously won back the governorship contributed an average of five percentage points more to its vote total than states controlled by the opposition. Finally, Enrique Peña Nieto's campaign for the presidency leaned heavily on his record as governor of the State of Mexico.[6] Without retaining that post, the candidate would not have had a record as an executive office-holder to tout.

The challenge of adaptation

Dominant parties that lose access to their hyper-incumbency advantages must adapt in order to survive. As the partisan playing field levels, giving opposition parties a greater probability of victory, dominant parties must transform themselves into standard competitors that win mainly on the basis of their policy offers and the quality of their candidates. If the level playing field yields an opposition victory at the national level, then formerly dominant parties face an even greater threat. Their loss of the executive means that state party organisations will only survive if they differentiate themselves from the national party by crafting state-specific platforms and nominating locally revered candidates.

Yet dominant parties are among the least well-equipped parties to adapt. They are built to administer single-party dominance, not to compete as one among equals. Their organisations are dedicated more to controlling local politics through subnational party units that do the national leaders' bidding than to representing local voters' demands. Indeed, dominant parties exert so much power that, in most cases, they mould their societies and set the parameters of party competition. Dominant parties are founded to control, not to adapt.

Existing literature from distinct theoretical traditions largely agrees that party adaptation only occurs under narrow circumstances, even for the most flexible parties. Scholars working in the historical institutionalist tradition argue that organisations stubbornly resist change for three reasons. First, parties' founding *raison d'être* infuses every aspect of the organisation's character, like a genetic code that cannot be reprogrammed.[7] Second, parties create durable linkages to their initial core constituencies that inhibit the subsequent incorporation of new groups later on.[8] Finally, like all organisations, parties create bureaucracies that are loath to give up power to new groups, even when doing so might allow the party to prosper.[9] These obstacles would imply that dominant parties established to coordinate among rival elites, that function as 'coalitions of the whole'[10] incorporating broad social sectors, and that administer politics in a non-competitive environment will not be able to adapt to the rigours of competition.

Where historical institutionalism sees only obstacles to adaptation, rationalist accounts open the possibility of party change, though not nearly as widely as many analysts' readings would suggest. For Downs,[11] parties only act rationally when all intra-party actors have the same goal, thus operating as a unified team.[12] Most empirical work on parties, however, shows deep disagreements between party factions that must be overcome in order to adapt.[13] Virtually all rationalist accounts assume that party leaders seek to maximise votes and thus are the most interested in responding to voters' preferences.[14] As a result, adaptation only occurs when leaders can impose their will, a process that analysts have documented for parties in Latin America[15] and Europe.[16]

Even if leaders are able to dominate other factions and spearhead reform processes among standard parties in competitive democracies, dominant parties are different. Their leaders are highly invested in maintaining central party control rather than giving lower-level units the independence to respond to local voters' demands. In fact, as we show below, if national leaders in the PRI had successfully controlled the reform process, the party would most likely have failed.

We argue that the PRI was only able to adapt because state party leaders wrested power from their national counterparts during Mexico's protracted transition to fully competitive democracy. State party leaders were better able to adapt to the rigours of competition and played a major role in resuscitating the party. Yet the process of moving from the old centralised form of dominant party organisation to the new form of greater decentralisation and enhanced power-sharing was not consensual. National party leaders attempted to impose their own model that would have *increased* centralisation. They ceded power to state party organisations only because political and economic circumstances forced their hand. In particular, national leaders' loss of politicised public resources and opposition party pressure led to reforms that gave state party organisations independent resources and transformed them into powerful actors within the PRI.

Centralised party organisation under PRI dominance

From its founding in 1929 until the 1990s, the PRI operated as a highly centralised party that sought to control state party organisations, manage social demands from citizens, and hold sway over politicians' career paths at all levels of the political system.

The dominant party itself, initially called the National Revolutionary Party (PNR), was formed by President Plutarco Elías Calles to manage tensions between various groups that were mobilised during the Revolution of 1910 and the subsequent civil war of the winners.[17] One of the party's main goals was to control the demands of social sectors, including peasants who had been armed and organised in an effort to crush the landed elite, and urban labour organisations then under the influence of anarchist and communist ideologies.[18] By the mid-1940s, the party had created a system of authoritarian corporatism that aggregated and mediated social demands through three non-competing sectoral organisations among urban labour, the peasantry and a somewhat amorphous urban 'popular' sector that included government employees and service-sector workers. The PRI used the state to subsidise these groups through direct resource transfers and laws that created closed shops, with recognition for official unions linked to the sectors.[19] As a result, each sector quickly came to dominate its own social group and incorporate these groups into the PRI through collective and compulsory membership in the party. Unlike societal corporatism practised in Scandinavian countries, authoritarian corporatism involved few mechanisms for the sectors to manoeuvre independently. Instead, they were tightly controlled by the sitting president, who could use them to manage social demands and, if such management failed, impose his own handpicked leaders, known as *charros*.

The other main rationale for creating an official party was to regulate relations between regional power-brokers known as *caciques* who had designs on state and national power. The system's three main mechanisms leaned more toward top-down control than power-sharing. First, single-party dominance requires special mechanisms for distributing power that differ from those in fully competitive democracies. Where elections are the main arbiter of who wins office, power flows up from the electorate, inducing politicians to appeal to voters to advance their careers. But in stable dominant party systems, it is a foregone conclusion that the incumbent party will win the next election. As a substitute for sovereign voters, Mexico's system endowed the president with substantial power, including the ability to nominate candidates. Under party dominance, nomination was tantamount to winning office, meaning that the president effectively controlled the career path of every PRI politician in the country.

Second, to limit the power of the presidency and discourage incumbents from remaining in office, which would effectively convert the dominant party system into a dictatorship, the regime adopted a constitutional provision against re-election and a norm of respecting those term limits.[20] As Magaloni writes, 'Regular succession gave potential rivals within the ruling coalition an incentive to wait for their turn instead of scheming assassinations against the sitting president and each other.'[21]

Finally, the dominant party exerted its control over state party organisations and their affiliated politicians.[22] Managing these relations was so important that the executive office created the Secretary of Government, widely known as the second most powerful official in Mexico, who was largely dedicated to this task. The process of subordinating state party organisations occurred quickly during the 1940s and 1950s in many states, as the president's access to overwhelming resources cowed recalcitrant factions.[23] So strong was his power that the president would sometimes impose his favoured candidate for governor despite local objections. As one indicator of this national-level imposition, Ibarra shows that nearly 40 per cent of the governors since 1929 in the six states he coded had political backgrounds more strongly associated with careers in national rather than state-level politics.[24] In some instances, a president would remove elected governors who conflicted with his interests.[25]

However, the president did not manage to subordinate all state party organisations. Camp writes that 'Despite the president's power, some states under each presidential administration have managed to dominate the selection of their own gubernatorial pre-candidate'.[26] Ibarra further shows that at least three states managed to retain significant local autonomy for many decades, including the State of Mexico, which produced the PRI's victorious presidential candidate in 2012.[27] We discuss the importance of these relatively more autonomous state party organisations for the PRI's comeback below.

Protracted transition to democracy and the new organisational model

Notwithstanding the anomalous state party organisations, the PRI's hierarchical national-level control over subnational party units, its affiliated politicians and broad sectors of society endured until the 1990s when rising political competition unsettled the old equilibrium. Two elements of Mexico's transition to fully competitive democracy merit special attention here. First, the transition itself was protracted, beginning after the 1982 debt crisis and culminating in the PRI's 2000 loss of the presidency. These nearly two decades of rising competition gave actors within the PRI time to negotiate a new organisational settlement. As the transition advanced, the relative power endowments of the party's national leadership and its affiliated state party organisations changed, creating the need for two major rounds of negotiation before a more stable settlement produced the new federalist organisational model.

Second, during the long transition to democracy, states became important arenas of competition between ascendant opposition parties and the PRI. As we describe in detail below, intensifying competition spurred PRI state party organisations to demand more and more autonomy from the centre and, eventually, to invert the historical relationship by controlling key aspects of the national party.

In this section, we provide what Bates referred to as an 'analytic narrative'[28] of the two rounds of negotiation between national and state party leaders in the PRI that ultimately led to the new settlement and the federalist organisational model. National leaders, including the president before 2000, wanted to maintain centralised control over subnational party units; state leaders wanted to wrest control away from Mexico City to determine their own fates. In examining the interaction between these actors, we pay attention to the changing political and economic conditions that affected their relative power endowments, generally weakening national leaders and strengthening local leaders as inter-party competition intensified. Much of the history we discuss is well known to scholars of Mexico's politics, but our reading of it is heavily influenced by the synthesis in Joy Langston's excellent book on the reform of the PRI and her prior body of work.[29]

Round 1: Aborted reform from above (1988–1995)

The first round of negotiations between the PRI's national leadership – then controlled firmly by the sitting president – and subnational party units occurred between 1988 and 1995. In this period, the main actors revealed their preferences for decentralising reforms or the continuation of centralised hierarchical control under somewhat different terms.[30] Although the president's power had been diminished owing to economic crisis and an ascendant opposition, he still maintained sufficient control over resources to impose his preference for continuity over reform.

The 1982 debt crisis was an unparalleled shock to the PRI. In the prior period from the 1950s to the 1970s, the party facilitated and oversaw such dramatic economic expansion that Mexico was considered a miraculous economic juggernaut.[31] The 1982 debt crisis was thus an alarming revelation of the PRI's economic mismanagement brought on by a decade of accumulated foreign debt. The crisis itself forced a major devaluation of the peso, which cut its value in half. Real wages fell by nearly 40 per cent and millions of Mexicans already in precarious economic circumstances plunged into poverty. The initial heterodox response failed and, by 1984, the administration embarked on an orthodox strategy that cut discretionary social spending in half and further tightened the screws on an ailing population.[32]

Though it was no surprise to students of economic voting theory,[33] the PRI was stunned by its lacklustre showing in the 1988 presidential election. A defector from the PRI's left wing and son of the party's founder, Cuauhtémoc Cárdenas, cobbled together a leftist coalition and may very well have beaten the PRI at the polls.[34] Massive fraud in the vote count either saved the PRI or padded its victory up to the razor-thin majority of 50.7 per cent.

The electoral 'scare,' as Langston calls it,[35] showed that the PRI needed to reform in order to remain viable. Two broad proposals emerged. On the one side, President Salinas sought to diminish the power of the party's allied sectoral organisations which had been established in the 1940s to incorporate the entire economically active population, then categorised as (formal) urban labour, peasants and the 'popular' sector which included government employees and service workers. The intervening four decades had changed Mexico's economy and the sectors no longer cast as wide a net over society. The rural economy had shrunk, the service sector had swelled, and the informal sector accounted for as much as a third of the economy. The president's reform initiative was to jettison the party sectors and substitute geographically defined party units. At first blush, this proposal would seem to have fulfilled the hopes of subnational party units that sought to enhance their influence. But Salinas's vision was to control this new party network from the presidential palace.

State party leaders put forth an alternative proposal for reform, one that would involve power-sharing between the president and state governors, all of whom were members of the PRI at the time. Recognising that the PRI was substantially funded by illicit public resources administered by the executive branch, they feared that losing the presidency in the subsequent 1994 elections without first decentralising the party apparatus would leave them unable to compete with rising challenger parties. Governors were also concerned about the more immediate fate of their state party organisations. Having lost the super-majority in Congress in 1988 and wanting to pass constitutional amendments to further aspects of his free-market reform agenda, President Salinas negotiated congressional votes for elected positions with the opposition PAN. The PRI's state party leaders were forced to concede nearly a dozen jurisdictions, including important municipalities and one governorship.[36] Regardless of whether they had won these positions through electoral malfeasance, they sought to repel what they viewed as an attack by their party leaders. One way to protect bastions was to force the president into a power-sharing agreement within the PRI.

The preferences of the two sides were manifest at the PRI 14th National Assembly held in 1990. The Salinas proposal for reform was welcomed, but the delegates, most of whom were handpicked by sitting governors, tried to take it much further and adopt decentralising reforms in pursuit of a power-sharing model.[37]

At the time, the presidency still commanded substantial resources that could be used to control the career paths of PRI politicians. Although the initial round of privatisations had diminished the depth of the public trough that the PRI plumbed for funds,[38] Salinas was able to generate partisan resources in two ways. First, the privatisations themselves, some amounting to billions of dollars, generated one-time resources that the president used to reinforce the PRI.[39] These monies made their way into an ambitious poverty-alleviation programme called PRONASOL,[40] which was administered with partisan bias.[41] Second, the president was able to generate resources of an even more discretionary nature by imploring the magnates who had benefited from the privatisations to contribute handsomely to the party.[42]

In this period, there was no oversight of campaign spending, no limits on contributions, and only token public party finance.[43] As a result, the PRI's resource advantages over opposition parties were substantial and thus discouraged most politicians from defecting from the party. If resource control was insufficient to manage some state party organisations, Salinas also retained the ability to decide elections. The administrative body in charge of counting votes was still firmly controlled by the executive branch.

Thus, although the PRI's state party organisations manifested their preference for a decentralising reform, their plan fell on deaf ears. The president had opened the door to reform at the party's 14th National Assembly, but when lower-level cadres tried to push it further, the president not only restored centralised hierarchical control, but he arguably enhanced it by transferring some of the fiscal resources the party would have administered to the federal government's vote-buying machine.[44]

Round 2: The new power-sharing agreement takes shape (1996–2000)

The relative power endowments of the president and state party leaders changed substantially from 1996 to 2000, weakening the de facto party leader and obliging him to concede substantial control over the party to his state-level co-partisans.[45] The new power-sharing organisation emerged as the PRI lost its simple majority in Congress in 1997 and in the shadow of its loss of the presidency in 2000. Ironically, it was the president's diminished power relative to state party leaders during this period that permitted the PRI to successfully negotiate the transition from dominant party to democratic player.

The president's influence over PRI politicians and, by extension, over state party organisations decreased in the mid- and late 1990s for three reasons. First, shortly after Ernesto Zedillo assumed the presidency in late 1994, Mexico experienced a short but dramatic economic crisis. Fearing a strong opposition challenge in the elections of that year, the outgoing president, Carlos Salinas, maintained an overvalued peso, which brought short-term benefits for broad constituencies, including businesses with dollar-denominated debt and wage-earners eager to avoid inflation. At the same time, Mexico experienced an expected but unsettling decline in short-term portfolio investment as financial interests accommodated themselves to the new North American Free Trade Agreement (NAFTA). The two processes combined to reveal weakness in the peso just after the 1994 elections. Although Salinas's gamble paid off, his use of the economy for political purposes spawned the first financial crisis of the new free-market era as investors who could now move their money with a mouse-click removed billions of dollars of liquid assets over a brief period. The government could not respond and inflation soared, plunging large portions of the emerging middle class into a debt spiral and further straining threadbare social programmes.[46]

The parallels to the 1982 debt crisis were not lost on PRI leaders. If they could not find resources to shore up electoral support through energetic campaigns and massive vote-buying efforts, as they had in the past, the party stood to suffer large losses at the polls.

The PRI could not simply increase its take from the federal public budget. By this time, privatisation had reduced the state's ownership of the economy from a high of 22.4 per cent of GDP in 1982 to just 8.6 per cent in 1996.[47] As a result, the PRI needed an alternative source of funding. In deference to its own financial needs and as a concession to the emboldened opposition parties, President Zedillo pushed through a consequential change to the election code in 1996 that made the PRI financially independent from the federal government for the first time in its history. Public financing for parties, which had been negligible just a few years earlier, now increased twelvefold, making Mexico's elections the most expensive in the world.[48] Strict new limits on private financing meant that public monies dominated. At the same time, the Federal Electoral Institute became fully independent of the government and was endowed with new powers of campaign finance oversight as well as the authority to sanction malfeasance.[49] Thus, as it funded itself through legitimate public funds, the PRI also paved the way for opposition parties to gain windfall financing far beyond what they had been able to raise from private sources in the decades since the initiation of single-party dominance.[50]

The marked decrease in resource asymmetries between the PRI and opposition parties levelled the playing field at a time when dissatisfaction with the party's economic performance threatened to spur large-scale voter dealignment. Both elements increased the urgency of party reform. State party leaders worried that a negative coat-tails effect would hurt them badly in upcoming gubernatorial elections and that, if the PRI lost the presidency in 2000 before the party decentralised its organisation, they would have little foundation on which to rebuild.[51] The president worried that the opposition parties' enhanced probability of winning might encourage PRI politicians to defect.[52]

The move to legitimate public party financing made the PRI fiscally independent from the executive branch for the first time in its history. Yet the party's national executive committee (CEN), which was still largely under the president's control, had wide discretion over how much money each state party organisation would receive.[53]

The decisive element that increased the power of the remaining 19 PRI-affiliated governors relative to the president was an increase in fiscal decentralisation. As Díaz-Cayeros narrates, states collected few taxes and, over the decades of single-party dominance, they transferred more and more fiscal power to the central government in exchange for resource-sharing agreements called 'participations'.[54] Yet each governor was required to negotiate the size of his state's allocation every year. Governors chafed under this centralising scheme but could do little to alter the arrangement when PRI dominance and hyper-presidentialism were unassailable.

If PRI-affiliated governors preferred enhanced fiscal federalism, then the opposition, which controlled 13 of 32 federal entities by 1998, demanded it. This unlikely alliance succeeded in renegotiating the terms of access to nominally federal resources. Following a 1998 change to the law, federal participations were allocated by formula rather than political considerations. These resources were a veritable gold mine for governors – what Langston refers to as the 'governors' perfect world'.[55] Although a goodly proportion of state budgets are not programmable, governors could use the excess for discretionary purposes. They encountered little oversight from the federal government and little restraint from their local legislatures.[56] Governors now had resources that were independent from both the president and the PRI's national leadership.

The combination of economic privatisations that reduced the PRI's access to illicit public resources, an increase in legitimate public party financing that brought greater resources for challenger parties, and fiscal decentralisation that gave governors independent financial wherewithal, had a major impact on the organisation of the PRI. Now the president was dramatically weakened and his state-level co-partisans notably strengthened to the point that some observers referred to governors as 'the new viceroys'.[57] In the shadow of its loss of the presidency in 2000, state party organisations were able to push through a party reform project oriented toward power-sharing between the centre and the states.

The new power-sharing arrangement devolved significant authority to the party's remaining governors, beginning in 1996 at the PRI's 17th National Assembly.[58] The authority they craved mostly concerned nominations for office.[59] Their control over large amounts of resources made them into indispensable campaign allies for the national party, forcing the latter to cede formal or informal power to them in influencing three types of nominations.

First, the governors were intensely interested in controlling the nominees to succeed them. In a trenchant analysis that relates what we have long known about presidential succession in Mexico[60] to gubernatorial politics, Langston argues that by picking their possible successors, governors could more easily control local factions while in office, avoid prosecution for malfeasance, and retain political influence after the end of their constitutionally mandated single term.[61] Over the next several years, the PRI experimented with selection methods for gubernatorial candidates, including handpicking them in the party's well-worn style or using open primaries. No matter which method was used, sitting governors were able to use their backroom influence with national party leaders or their discretionary resources for electioneering to help decide on the nominee.

Second, the governors' influence over the PRI's nominees for their state's congressional delegation expanded. Governors could now dedicate significant resources to local campaigns, and the national party leadership reasoned that they would have more incentive to do so if they influenced the slate of candidates. Once again, the party's nomination methods for plurality district candidates varied over the next several years. When primary elections were employed, governors often used their influence to ensure that only one candidate per constituency appeared on the ballot.[62]

Third, the governors prised open the process of selecting the PRI's nominee for the presidency, a process that was so mysterious and arcane that Jorge Castañeda's exploration of the subject was subtitled 'The archeology of presidential succession in Mexico'.[63] The rules adopted in 1996 and put in place for the 2000 contest simply stated that the nominee must have held a prior elected office. Bureaucrats, no matter how close to the sitting president, could no longer be nominated. Governors would now have a strong argument that the nominee should come from among their ranks. They hold the highest executive office below the president, they can point to an immediate past record in office, and they command resources that give them advantages in their home state. It is no surprise, then, that the PRI's nominees for president in all elections since the reform have been governors.

In sum, a decline in the resource endowment of the president relative to PRI-affiliated governors in the mid-1990s emboldened state party organisations, allowing them to renegotiate the distribution of power within the party. The new organisation dispensed with nearly seven decades of presidential dominance and substituted a power-sharing arrangement that we call the strategy of federalism.

The new power-sharing agreement did not mark the end of factional rivalries in the PRI – these naturally flared in the wake of the PRI's loss of the presidency in 2000.[64] However, the settlement ironed out during Mexico's protracted transition to fully competitive democracy created a formal and informal framework for subsequent negotiations. This new framework put state party organisations on even terms with national party leaders, a change that we believe saved the party from electoral failure after its loss of the presidency. We explore this claim in the next section.

Party reform and the PRI's comeback

Party reform facilitated the PRI's transformation from a dominant party into a viable competitor in Mexico's fully competitive democracy. We suspect that had the party remained hierarchical and centralised under the control of the president until the fateful 2000 elections, the PRI would have lost gubernatorial elections over the next several years in the 19 states where it then held power. Political control from Mexico City without concomitant resources flowing to state party organisations would have left local PRI affiliates sufficiently poor and dejected that candidates might have defected to the rising opposition. Those that remained would have been subject to the nominating criteria of the national party, which may not have responded as effectively as locally embedded operatives to voters' demands. If the national leadership had remained firmly in control, we speculate that the PRI would have fared poorly, becoming a withered shell or disappearing with the dominant party system it created.

Our speculation is based on counterfactual reasoning, because we cannot observe a world in which the PRI failed to reform and subsequently lost elections. However, we can examine related variation across states. Although all states experienced the shifting balance of power from the national to state party organisations as the same time in the mid- to late 1990s, some states were better equipped to take advantage of the change than others. A handful of state party organisations managed to wrest more autonomy from the national party than others even before the new power-sharing organisation was established.[65] Ibarra argues that in these states, local factions learned how to accommodate each other through negotiation, whereas in states without prior experience of autonomy from the federal government, factions were in open conflict in the 1990s and 2000s.[66] Thus, as the federalist strategy was put in motion, states with accommodative factionalism were better able to pour their energies into campaigning behind a consensus nominee for the governorship, whereas states with conflictual factionalism occupied themselves with internecine battles and suffered defections of key politicians.

In service of this argument, Ibarra coded the degree of factionalism among PRI state party organisations for 58 gubernatorial elections from 1995 to 2010, categorising them as accommodative, conflictual, or intermediary.[67] He then examined the impact of factionalism on the PRI's performance as measured by the vote share margin between it and the largest challenger. This variable thus takes on positive values when the PRI wins and negative values when it loses. The model controls for the vote share obtained by the PRI in the prior gubernatorial election so that it isolates the impact of factionalism on the change in the party's vote share from prior to the current election. To account for alternative arguments for the PRI's performance relative to the opposition, the model also includes measures of the sitting governor's popularity, the state level of socio-economic status, the amount of federal participations, the governor's access to discretionary resources, and the proportion of the economically active population that belonged to a union associated with the PRI's labour sector.

The effect of factionalism was substantial, even when controlling for variables associated with other plausible causes of variation in the PRI's electoral performance. In states where factions accommodated each other, the PRI was predicted to win 16.3 percentage points more than where factions were in conflict. By comparison, a sitting PRI governor would have to raise his approval rating among voters by a whopping 58 points to help his party's nominee as much as accommodative factionalism would.

We offer brief case studies of the PRI's organisation and its electoral fortunes in two states to help bolster and interpret the quantitative findings. The central-western state of Michoacán played an important role in Mexico's transition to multi-party democracy. From 1980 to 1986, it was governed by Cuauhtémoc Cárdenas, then a member of the PRI, who defected from the dominant party to challenge its 1988 candidate for the presidency, Carlos Salinas. Though Cárdenas lost in the official polling, he subsequently founded the leftist PRD, which played a major role in pushing Mexico's democratisation forward.[68] Yet despite the fact that Michoacán was home base for the PRD, the PRI won every gubernatorial election until 2002.

The 1995 contest provides an excellent example of the importance of factional unity for the PRI's staying power. Pre-election conditions in that year seemed to favour the opposition. The crushing 1994 economic crisis was just a year old and opinion polls showed that the PRI's nominee – Manuel Tinoco Rubí – was less popular than his intra-party rivals.[69] At the same time, the candidate for the left – Cristóbal Arias Solís – had served as Governor Cárdenas's right-hand man and the PAN's candidate – Felipe Calderón – was such an able campaigner that he went on to become president in 2006. Public opinion polls at the outset of the campaigns showed a dead heat between the top candidates, yet the PRI's candidate won by 6.5 percentage points.

Ibarra argues that accommodative factionalism was the key to the PRI's victory.[70] Despite the opposition's popularity, there were no splits and the leaders of the main factions supported Tinoco, thus allowing the party to focus on electioneering rather than infighting, and conveying an image of professionalism, reliability and strength rather than uncertainty. The party achieved unity by forging pre-election agreements to distribute administrative appointments and other spoils of office among the competing factions, a process that Ibarra attributes to the state party's relative autonomy from the national organisation in the two decades prior to Tinoco's successful bid for the governorship.[71]

By contrast, PRI factions were in open conflict in the run-up to the 1998 gubernatorial election in the northern state of Zacatecas. Unlike in Michoacán, factional unity in Zacatecas seemed over-determined. The party held a 44-percentage-point advantage in pre-election polls, suggesting that defection would be futile.[72] Yet when the state party, under the tutelage of national PRI leaders, nominated Marco Antonio Olvera, who had proven less popular in internal polls, Ricardo Monreal Ávila left to run as the candidate of the PRD. The split was public and marked by hostile personal attacks that presumably did not play well with voters. In just 17 days between the announced split and Monreal's official nomination with the PRD, the PRI's massive advantage disappeared. On election day, Monreal won the governorship by 6.1 percentage points, giving the PRD a high-level office that it could not have attained otherwise.

If the PRI's state party organisation had managed to keep Monreal in the fold, it very likely would have retained the governorship. We cannot know whether Monreal could have been retained, but Ibarra argues that the PRI in Zacatecas was incapable of reaching consensus in the face of discord.[73] Unlike in Michoacán, the state party in Zacatecas had relied on PRI presidents to enforce local discipline in the decades before the 1998 debacle. As a result, local party factions lacked the tools to negotiate effectively with one another, falling back on recriminations and threats when consensus was not apparent.

We believe that the key to local electoral success for the PRI is rooted in the combination of relative local autonomy from the national party and the ability of local party leaders to maintain unity through accommodative agreements. The talent for reaching such agreements is not unique to the state parties that have had decades of practice in managing their own affairs, as in the example of Michoacán; rather, early relative autonomy simply permitted such state party organisations to take advantage of the new federalist style of party organisation in the mid- to late 1990s. Subsequently, other state party organisations have learned to accommodate the interests of rival factions and, as a result, the PRI began to rebound from 2002 on, winning 16 governorships by 2012 and positioning itself to take back the presidency in that year.

Conclusion

Dominant parties that face rising competition are threatened not only with losing office, but with disappearing. Although dominant parties in presidential systems win by higher vote margins, on average, than those in parliamentary systems,[74] the former may be more vulnerable than the latter. In the face of economic strains, corruption scandals or other events that increase voters' dissatisfaction with the dominant incumbent party, a single popular opposition candidate may be able to obtain the presidency. If this happens, dominant parties may quickly lose their remaining hold over subnational offices, wiping them from the political scene.

In this chapter, we have shown how Mexico's long-dominant PRI avoided this fate by pursuing the strategy of federalism and decentralising its party organisation during the protracted transition to democracy before it lost the presidency in 2000. In doing so, the party developed a power-sharing settlement between national and state-level leaders, allowing the latter to nominate local candidates and craft local platforms that were presumably more responsive to local voters' demands. This more decentralised form of party organisation effectively saved the party from disappearing at the onset of democratisation and helped it rebuild national prominence, enabling it to reclaim the presidency in 2012.

We stress, however, that the strategy of federalism was not born of consensus between national and state leaders; rather, the latter had to wrest power from the former in iterated negotiations that shifted as broader political and economic conditions altered the power endowments of the two sets of actors. National leaders strongly resisted decentralising reforms and managed to block them until the mid- to late 1990s. Had they resisted until the party lost the presidency in 2000, we suspect that the PRI would have quickly lost subnational offices and its survival would have been threatened. Thus, the reform process saved the party from itself.

Mexico's experience suggests that dominant parties facing rising competition should follow the strategy of federalism and pre-emptively decentralise their organisations. This conclusion, however, is conditional in our view, because decentralisation carries the risk that locally powerful politicians will defect to form their own parties. Why, for instance, did the PRI remain intact rather than splitting into smaller regional parties? In other countries, such as Peru, the fiscal power of regional office-holders has militated against party aggregation to such an extent that there are virtually no parties with national-level projection. Thus, implementing federalist party organisation is a risky strategy that could have dire consequences for other dominant parties unless elements are in place to encourage party aggregation across geographic constituencies.

In Mexico, four elements continued to give national PRI leaders strength and discouraged the wholesale defection of regionally powerful governors to start their own parties. First, the power of the president has encouraged cross-district aggregation to win the national prize.[75] Second, ballot access in Mexico requires running on a party label, and party registration requires a presence in 65 per cent of states as well as a national three per cent vote threshold to maintain registration. Third, although PRI governors wrested control from the national party to nominate plurality candidates for Congress, Mexico uses a mixed system that also includes 40 per cent of candidacies through closed-list proportional representation, which is controlled by the national party. Finally, national party organisations continue to receive public financing and, following the 2007 reform, the system prohibits all private, candidate and party financing of election campaigns. These substantial powers for national party central committees mean that regional power-brokers cannot easily mount effective challenges by starting new parties, but prosper instead through a more decentralised power-sharing arrangement.

If dominant parties can navigate the balance between centralisation and decentralisation, decentralising enough to enhance local electoral competitiveness but remaining centralised enough to continue as a single, integrated party, they can position themselves well to survive the demands of fully competitive democracy.

4

Power, patronage and politics in Malaysia: UMNO's dominant state?

Edmund Terence Gomez

In May 2013, following a highly contentious and closely fought general election, Malaysia's ruling coalition, the Barisan Nasional (BN, or National Front), lost the popular vote but retained power only because it had managed to secure more seats in parliament than the opposition coalition, the Pakatan Rakyat (PR, or People's Coalition). After this election, one party in the ruling coalition, the United Malays National Organization (UMNO), retained hegemony over the political system in spite of its steadily diminishing capacity to muster strong electoral support.

UMNO has been the single dominant force in Malaysian politics since independence in 1957, despite its claim that, through a consociational framework, it shares power with a dozen or so parties in the BN.[1] This dominance flows from the subservience of the other BN parties to UMNO, as many of them depend on this Malay-based party to win seats. UMNO has always held the largest number of seats in parliament, won during free – though not fair – elections. Regular and free elections have enabled the opposition to capture control of state governments in the Malaysian federation. But, to retain federal power, the BN has persistently resorted to highly racialised political discourses, propagated through its control of the mainstream media, as well as unfair practices such as abuse of its access to extensive funding and government machinery to dispense money, services and infrastructure projects.[2] Malaysia is for this reason regarded as a 'quasi-authoritarian', 'semi-democratic' or 'competitive authoritarian' state.[3] In spite of this hold over federal power, UMNO's influence in society has been steadily eroding, as can be seen in the overwhelming rejection of the party by the urban middle class and a large segment of rural Malays, long its primary support base.

UMNO's persistent hegemony, despite a steady erosion of support, presents a puzzle about the political system as well as the relationship between the state and a society that has rapidly modernised and that now includes an intelligent and demanding middle class. The party's enduring rule is not merely due to a deeply flawed electoral system characterised by serious gerrymandering and malapportionment of constituencies. After all, in 1999, following another contentious and deeply divisive general election, UMNO lost considerable support in rural constituencies in the peninsula, but retained the vote of the urban middle class; in Malaysia's highly gerrymandered system, such results could have worked in favour of the opposition. In 2013, UMNO was overwhelmingly rejected by the urban middle class but it regained sufficient support in rural constituencies to (barely) retain power.

To understand UMNO's persistent hegemony, Malaysian politics have to be evaluated in terms of two key issues: policies and institutions. A historical analysis of the outcomes of policies to promote industrialisation along with a review of electoral trends over the past two decades provides insights into how UMNO has sustained its dominant position in politics in the face of eroding support, while also drawing attention to the significance and conduct of coalition politics, specifically those of the opposition.

Developmental policies, patronage and the new middle class

Malaysia offers an intriguing study of rapid industrialisation through an extensive mix of policies involving a highly interventionist state along with the adoption of non-interventionist neoliberal ideas, including extensive privatisation of government entities. Another dimension

Table 1: Ownership of share capital (at par value) of limited companies, 1969–2008 (expressed as percentages)

	1969	1970	1975	1980	1985	1990	1995	1999	2004	2006	2008
Bumiputera individuals & trust agencies	1.5	2.4	9.2	12.5	19.1	19.2	20.6	19.1	18.9	19.4	21.9
Chinese	22.8	27.2	n.a.	n.a.	33.4	45.5	40.9	37.9	39.0	42.4	34.9
Indians	0.9	1.1	n.a.	n.a.	1.2	1.0	1.5	1.5	1.2	1.1	1.6
Other	–	–	–	–	–	–	–	0.9	0.4	0.4	0.1
Nominee companies	2.1	6.0	n.a.	n.a.	1.3	8.5	8.3	7.9	8.0	6.6	3.5
Locally controlled firms	10.1	–	–	–	7.2	0.3	1.0	–	–	–	–
Foreigners	62.1	63.4	53.3	42.9	26.0	25.4	27.7	32.7	32.5	30.1	37.9

Source: Malaysia, *Tenth Malaysia Plan, 2011–2015* (Kuala Lumpur, 2010)

of this unique policy regime has been affirmative action, which was introduced in 1970, and which determined who would receive privatised rents.

A defining characteristic of Malaysia's development model since the early 1980s has been the high degree of government intervention in the economy. Known as the 'developmental state',[4] this has as its core features an autonomous state system with the capacity to deliver social and economic policies; a coherently structured industrial policy to foster entrepreneurial private firms through selective patronage; state-controlled financial institutions to fund this development; and a well-functioning education system that has groomed human capital to operate this economy.[5]

While there was widespread acceptance by the BN of features of a developmental state, in the mid-1980s political leaders came to be inspired by a vastly different model of development – neoliberalism, based on the ideas of Friedrich Hayek. Neoliberalism advocated the need for limiting state intervention in the economy and extolled the virtues of allowing the private sector to drive growth.[6] Its tenets include policies that restrain labour rights and check the growth of the welfare state.

The tenets on which the developmental state and neoliberalism are based are at opposite ends of the policy spectrum, but they share a common feature: the close nexus between state and business. In Malaysia, this state–business linkage was created to nurture domestic enterprises through a system of selective patronage. The evolution of this state–business nexus offers insights into the conduct of political power and patronage in UMNO.[7]

The need for a system of selective patronage (which has fostered and embedded state–business ties in UMNO) has been attributed to the socio-economic injustices created during British colonial rule. A decade after independence in 1957, public criticism emerged among Malay elites of the inadequate reforms instituted by UMNO to redress the marginalisation of this community under British rule in capitalist sectors of the economy. The wealth and income disparities between ethnic groups that had resulted contributed to race riots in 1969.[8] One response to this crisis was the introduction in 1970 of the 20-year New Economic Policy (NEP), based on affirmative action, to eradicate poverty and redress inequitable wealth distribution between the predominantly Malay Bumiputera ('sons of the soil') and other ethnic groups.[9] This was to be achieved through the redistribution of corporate equity along ethnic lines. In 1969 Bumiputera ownership of corporate equity stood at a mere 1.5 per cent (see Table 1). With the introduction of the NEP, governance and policy frameworks shifted toward much stronger and more centralised state control and aggressive redistributive interventions to increase Bumiputera participation in the corporate world.[10]

During the first decade of the NEP, the policy had two key dimensions. The first focused on education. Poor rural Malays were sent to well-equipped residential schools and then on to local and foreign universities, with government scholarships. The provision of sound education for this poor community as a means to achieve social mobility proved a phenomenal success, resulting in the rise of a new, independent Malay middle class while reducing poverty appreciably. This success of the NEP would garner UMNO immense rural support.

The NEP's second dimension, described as 'trusteeship',[11] entailed government intervention in the economy through public enterprises and trust agencies to accumulate capital on behalf of the Bumiputeras. These agencies, endowed with substantial public funds, acquired big businesses, a process aided by a government requirement that every quoted firm had to ensure that at least 30 per cent of its equity was allocated to Bumiputera agencies or individuals. Public enterprises, now called government-linked companies (GLCs), soon captured a huge share of firms in all major sectors: plantations, mining, manufacturing, services, banking, insurance and finance, and construction and property development.

This model of developing Bumiputera capital was changed by Mahathir Mohamad when he was appointed prime minister in 1981, a position he would hold for the next two decades. The ever-pragmatic Mahathir evolved a mix of developmental measures, such as affirmative action-driven enterprise development, government-led heavy industrialisation and the privatisation of key state enterprises. Mahathir also voiced his intent to selectively cultivate a cluster of entrepreneurial Malay capitalists in charge of well-diversified conglomerates with an international presence. He defended his selective form of patronage on the grounds that after ten years of the NEP, though the volume of corporate holdings held in the name of Bumiputeras had increased appreciably to 12.5 per cent, little progress had been made in developing private Malay entrepreneurs in control of big businesses (see Table 1).[12] This was the commencement of a patronage system that would define his premiership and become a constituent feature of UMNO-led governments.

From the mid-1980s, a sweeping privatisation programme was carried out to develop these new corporate captains, officially known as the Bumiputera Commercial and Industrial Community (BCIC) policy. Privatisation would facilitate Bumiputera capital accumulation. Those privy to such rents had a triple role – to be profit-oriented, drive industrialisation and develop Malay-owned small- and medium-scale enterprises (SMEs).[13] This wave of privatisations to rapidly create

Malay-owned conglomerates peaked between 1991 and 1995.

As affirmative action warranted privatised rent transfers to Bumiputeras, government leaders would contend that since the private sector, not public enterprises, had now become the main vehicle for economic development, the practice of political patronage and rent-seeking would be checked. However, privatisation saw the development of extensive clientelistic ties involving key UMNO leaders because of the absence of an independent and accountable monitoring body to ensure the transparent implementation of the policy.[14] By the mid-1990s, most large Bumiputera-controlled firms were linked to one of the three most powerful politicians of the time – Prime Minister Mahathir, Deputy Prime Minister Anwar Ibrahim and Daim Zainuddin, an economic adviser who had also served as finance minister between 1984 and 1990.[15] The concentration of access to privatised resources in the hands of a few politicians contributed to the rise of personalised politics, which exacerbated in turn UMNO factionalism.[16]

Mahathir's plans to develop Malay entrepreneurs quickly crumbled when the 1997 Asian currency crisis arose. Well-connected businesses that had obtained substantial loans from state-owned banks to buy their way to conglomeration found themselves severely over-leveraged and had to be bailed out by the GLCs. The bail-outs were also instituted to prevent a collapse of the financial system. In the process, national policy was drastically reversed, with a renewed emphasis being placed on state ownership. Before he retired in 2003 as prime minister, Mahathir publicly admitted that his policy endeavours had failed and that affirmative action-based patronage had resulted in a 'crutch mentality'.[17]

Another factor contributed to the fall of well-connected firms after the crisis. The fortunes of the well-connected depended on whether their patrons remained in power. After a serious feud between Mahathir and Anwar, the latter was removed from office in September 1998. Anwar's associates subsequently struggled to protect their corporate interests; many of them are no longer prominent in business. Similarly, when Daim fell out with Mahathir in 2001, the corporate assets of his allies and proxies were taken over by GLCs.[18]

Abdullah Ahmad Badawi, prime minister from 2003 to 2009, advocated policies markedly different from Mahathir's. While he retained a developmentalist model that would help foster Bumiputera capital, he had little interest in developing Malay – or Malaysian – big businesses. He nurtured SMEs, including cottage industries dealing with halal products, dominated by poor rural Malays, as well as Islamic-based financial services, as he believed that firms in these sectors had export capacity potential if developed well.[19]

This was an astute policy move, as the 2005 census of the corporate sector revealed that SMEs constituted about 99.2 per cent of all business establishments. SMEs then employed 5.6 million workers and contributed about 32 per cent of real GDP. But here, too, selective patronage was practised when SME programmes were implemented. For example, when the government created links between SMEs and transnational corporations (TNCs), Chinese firms were seldom allowed access to the domestic and overseas markets that these foreign companies offered. Domestic firms left out of these SME–TNC associations were capable of producing better-quality products at a cheaper rate, which would have helped them break into foreign markets. Such selective patronage that denied local entrepreneurial firms the opportunity to expand subsequently undermined the relationship between TNCs and SMEs, when the SMEs produced poor-quality products.

When Najib Razak replaced Abdullah as prime minister, he was confronted not merely with a political crisis – the BN had fared poorly in the 2008 general election – but also with a profound economic downturn precipitated by the global financial crisis, which plainly revealed the problems associated with neoliberalism. This crisis drew attention to grave structural problems, compelling Najib to assemble a team of specialists to fashion a 'new economic model' to foster 'sustainability' and 'inclusiveness'.[20] What had become patently obvious during the recession was the need to liberalise longstanding ethnic quota regulations involving corporate equity ownership, specifically so as to improve domestic investments, which had been in rapid decline since 1999 with the continued implementation of affirmative action.

The government subsequently released a series of plans, including the New Economic Model,[21] whose primary goal was the introduction of a 'new model' of development, one devoid of 'rent-seeking and patronage'. However, Najib's new model clearly persisted with Mahathir's mix of neoliberal and developmental state ideas in combination with affirmative action. When the government tried to review its longstanding position on affirmative action to promote domestic investments, Najib encountered serious protests from his own UMNO members. A core criticism was that deregulation would permit greater foreign presence in a developing economy still in the process of nurturing domestic enterprises. Embedded in Najib's development plans was the idea of a government confronting a serious dilemma: the need to remove race-based policies while pursuing the goal of increasing Bumiputera-owned corporate equity.

However, Malaysians requiring affirmative action have had little access to shares newly quoted on the stock exchange; this equity went to those who knew how to get them – hardly those constituting the poor. With the implementation of affirmative action, inter-ethnic wealth inequality was reduced, but intra-ethnic inequality among Bumiputeras had worsened. Serious allegations of corruption and conflict of interest emerged when much of this equity was channelled to well-connected Malays, who quickly sold out at a huge premium. Of the RM54 billion worth of quoted stock channelled to Bumiputeras since 1971, only RM2 billion of it remained in their hands by 2009.[22]

The resistance to the policy changes proposed by Najib was largely due to the patronage mechanism that had been created and embedded in UMNO. In turn, this has contributed to persistent factionalism in the party, which has threatened UMNO's hegemony within the political system.

New opposition, hard-fought elections and state–society mismatch

Mahathir's development model, focusing on heavy industrialisation, privatisation and big business, began to have a detrimental impact on

UMNO's rural Malay support from the late 1980s. This trend was first noted during the 1990 general election when BN registered a decline in votes in the poor Malay heartland states of Kelantan, Terengganu and Kedah. In 1990 BN faced serious competition from an opposition alliance created by the former finance minister Razaleigh Hamzah, comprising his UMNO faction, now registered as a political party named Parti Semangat 46 (Spirit of 46 Party) – UMNO was formed in 1946 – and an Islamic party, Parti Islam SeMalaysia (PAS). When in UMNO, Razaleigh had alleged that wealth concentration through selective patronage had led to the creation of a politically aligned 'new rich'.[23] Razaleigh would mount two unsuccessful electoral challenges, first in 1987 against Mahathir for the UMNO presidency, which he narrowly lost, and then as an opposition leader during the 1990 general election. Razaleigh's coalition would help PAS secure control of the Kelantan state government in this election.

Confronted with this strong challenge in the Malay heartland, UMNO realised the importance of becoming a 'responsive state'[24] if it hoped to retain power through the electoral process. Since Mahathir was reluctant to change his policy direction, he focused on garnering non-Malay and urban middle-class support. Mahathir introduced Vision 2020, an attempt to be inclusive by promoting a *Bangsa Malaysia*, loosely defined by him as a united Malaysian people. He also liberalised the economy by awarding huge privatised rents to non-Malays, claiming he now wanted to create 'Malaysian' conglomerates; lifted a ban on lion dance performances during the Chinese New Year; and allowed for the establishment of private universities to cater to well-qualified non-Bumiputeras who were unable to secure tertiary education in public institutions because of ethnically based entry quotas under affirmative action. These policy changes helped BN secure in the 1995 general election its most successful electoral victory. Although it obtained 65 per cent of the popular vote, it continued to lose Malay support, even though the economy had grown phenomenally over the previous five years, a factor contributing to the unprecedented non-Malay swing to the BN. After this election, Razaleigh disbanded his party and returned to UMNO, voicing discontent with PAS's Islamic policy agenda. PAS, however, retained control of the Kelantan state government.

In September 1998 a mass-based *reformasi* (reformation) movement emerged in protest over Mahathir's controversial dismissal of Anwar as deputy prime minister and UMNO deputy president and Anwar's subsequent arrest under what were widely believed to be trumped-up charges of sexual impropriety and corruption. While Anwar had appeared to be undermining Mahathir's handling of the economy after the 1997 currency crisis, the manner of his public humiliation and prosecution visibly revealed the subservience of the media, police and judiciary to the executive. Anwar's dismissal helped bring NGO activists into mainstream politics through the formation of Parti Keadilan Nasional (Keadilan, or Malaysian National Justice Party), whose members included an UMNO faction. A rainbow coalition was then formed that united Keadilan with socialists and Islamists. This coalition, Barisan Alternatif (BA, or Alternative Front), included PAS and the multi-ethnic, though predominantly Chinese-based, Democratic Action Party (DAP). Anwar was declared BA's de facto leader, though he would remain in prison until 2004.

In the 1999 general election, an 'ambivalence' was noted among the electorate in their support for either the BN or BA; the new opposition coalition was evidently not seen as a viable alternative by many Malaysians.[25] Bumiputera support for UMNO declined even further in the economically less-developed Malay-majority constituencies, though BN maintained this community's support in southern areas of the peninsula, suggesting intra-ethnic class differences. BN lost badly in the Malay-dominant states in the north and another state, Terengganu, fell to PAS. DAP, however, won only one additional parliamentary seat in 1999 compared to 1995, in spite of a decline in Chinese support for BN. DAP leaders were aware before the elections that it could win big or lose big and it lost big, clearly drawing reference to the outcome of their party's participation in the BA. Two years later, DAP left BA, citing longstanding differences with PAS over its Islamic state agenda.

PAS benefited most in the 1999 election because of intra-ethnic

Malay splits, winning control of two state governments, Terengganu and Kelantan. But the results indicated that any opposition coalition encompassing PAS would not be able to muster much support in a majority of parliamentary constituencies. PAS commanded little support in the southern industrialised states of Malacca, Negeri Sembilan and Johor. In Sabah and Sarawak, PAS had even less support. Protests against Mahathir's policies were the primary reason for PAS's electoral gains, not its espousal of the need for an Islamic state. BN's victory was also due to BA's inability to articulate a common vision that could unify Malaysians. Keadilan's alliance with PAS hindered the former's capacity to secure non-Malay support: even prominent Keadilan leaders acknowledged the repercussions of PAS's theocratic brand of politics.

Recognising rural Bumiputera discontent with economic policies and urban discontent with power concentration and corruption, before the 2004 general election BN, now under Abdullah, began articulating reforms that had been demanded by BA. Abdullah stated his intent to create a more inclusive society through his concept of *Islam Hadhari* (Islamic civilisation), a moderate vision compared with PAS's Islamic state. Abdullah's espousal of Islam Hadhari and his move to check corruption were well received by the urban middle class, while his policy intent to alleviate the plight of poor rural communities pleased the electorate in the Malay heartland and the two Borneo states.

BN recorded a major victory in 2004, obtaining 64 per cent of the popular support, which secured about 90 per cent of the seats in parliament. BN retained urban middle-class support and successfully recaptured considerable ground in the Malay heartland which it had lost to BA, bucking the trend of declining rural Malay support since 1990. Terengganu was recaptured, though Kelantan was lost by a mere seat to PAS. Abdullah's policies had resonated strongly with the rural poor who had long been marginalised by Mahathir's development policies.[26]

PAS's parliamentary performance was dismal, retaining only seven of its 27 seats. Six of these victories were in Kelantan. PAS's sole partner in the BA, Keadilan, did similarly badly, winning just one of the 58 seats it contested, Anwar's constituency. DAP, now out of the BA, secured two more seats; it clearly had more electoral support when not in coalition with PAS.

Once in power, Abdullah's inability to carry out his reforms, including the eradication of poverty, reduction in corruption and improvement of public sector efficiency, would cost him dearly in the 2008 general election. His attempt to de-racialise UMNO politics had also failed. In the economy, Abdullah had not been able to nurture entrepreneurial SMEs, bringing into question the practice of selective patronage and the effectiveness of race-based targeting.[27] With the opposition in disarray after 2004, UMNO members saw no need to check patronage and rent-seeking. To his detriment, Abdullah was seen to be cultivating his own clique of well-connected businesspeople. Corporate scandals were exposed involving his brother, son and son-in-law.

In 2008, BN registered considerable loss of popular support. Its presence in parliament was reduced by nearly 30 percentage points, down to 63 per cent. In state-level elections, for the first time in history, the opposition won more seats than the BN in five states: Kelantan, Kedah, Penang, Selangor and Perak (the last three states are among the most industrialised in the peninsula, while the first two are among the poorest).[28] BN obtained only 51.2 per cent of the popular vote and UMNO's presence in parliament fell from 109 seats to 79, a shock for a party accustomed to holding more than half. BN registered a massive double-digit fall in Chinese support, particularly in urban constituencies, and lost in nearly all Malay-majority constituencies, which indicated a constant swing in the Malay heartland between UMNO and PAS. Unlike UMNO, PAS had instituted changes to win back lost support after its thrashing in the 2004 election. It had begun to emphasise the promotion of a welfare state, not an Islamic state, a key factor that helped it regain much of the support it had lost to UMNO.

In the peninsula, BN obtained a mere 49.8 per cent of the total votes cast, meaning that the opposition had more popular support in this part of Malaysia.[29] Serious factionalism had contributed to UMNO's electoral performance. Party members reportedly sabotaged their own candidates for fear that if they secured ascendancy in UMNO, they would channel state rents to themselves. Abdullah was blamed for UMNO's poor performance and was forced to step down as prime minister.

Since the opposition had, collectively, won sufficient seats in five states to form the government, Keadilan, PAS and DAP combined forces once again to form a new coalition, Pakatan Rakyat (PR), after the general election. The possibility of ruling five states was too compelling for DAP to forgo joining this coalition.

To counter PR's multi-ethnic image, Prime Minister Najib actively marketed his *1Malaysia* slogan, ostensibly to unify the nation through trans-ethnic politics, and endorsed numerous policies to address the plight of poor Bumiputeras and counter the global financial crisis. However, Najib's policy reforms persisted with race-based initiatives, for a number of reasons. Regional cleavages had emerged, with deep poverty rampant in rural areas in Bumiputera-majority states, including Sabah, Kelantan, Perlis and Kedah, where the opposition had secured a strong presence. If his policies did not explicitly mention that Bumiputera economic interests would be protected and promoted, Najib feared UMNO's Malay support would be put in jeopardy in rural areas. Since these regional and social inequities had emerged because of an abuse of provisions within race-based policies, Najib also promised to end rent-seeking and patronage.

But several problems emerged, undermining Najib's pledge to check rent-seeking. Major corporate scandals were exposed involving three government-linked bodies, all cases where well-connected businesspeople and prominent BN politicians had secured lucrative rents. A range of public enterprises, including the Penang Port, had been privatised to one individual, Syed Mokhtar Al-Bukhary, who was aligned with Mahathir. UMNO in Sabah had covertly received an RM40-million donation from one individual, while Sarawak's then chief minister, Taib Mahmud, and his family were criticised for having amassed enormous wealth through an abuse of the state's vast resources.

In April 2013, having had four years to implement his policies, Najib dissolved parliament. BN's election manifesto spoke of the reforms in Najib's numerous government plans that he wanted to continue, but the results of the election indicated an electorate unconvinced by his transformation agenda. BN fared even worse in this election, securing only 133 parliamentary seats compared to the 140 it had obtained previously. UMNO fared better, though, winning 88 parliamentary seats, nine more than it had previously held, while it also emerged as the party with the largest presence in the lower house. BN registered huge defeats in urban middle-class constituencies, securing national victory only because of its support in Sabah and Sarawak; and it gained just a little more support than PR in the Malay heartland. BN lost the popular vote, obtaining only 49 per cent of electoral support nationally and 43 per cent in the peninsula. PR retained control of Selangor and Penang and made huge inroads in Johor – three of Malaysia's most industrialised states – while also maintaining its rule in Kelantan.

In 2013 PR, having shown it had the capacity to govern at state levels, went into the election confident of securing federal power, in spite of the gerrymandering and malapportionment that favoured BN. However, while PR secured immense support in urban industrialised states where the middle class demanded political and socio-economic reforms, the Malay heartland was fairly equally divided between BN and PR. PR managed to retain control of three states, Penang, Selangor and Kelantan, but lost control of Kedah and failed narrowly to wrest control of Perak and Terengganu, suggesting problems with its own form of governance. From a policy perspective, PR had, interestingly enough, not managed to offer a mode of development different from that proposed by Najib in his New Economic Model. In fact, when this plan was presented in parliament by the prime minister, Anwar reacted angrily by arguing that the BN had stolen his ideas. This was not surprising, as the New Economic Model was basically a reconstitution of Mahathir's mix-and-match development plan, and Anwar had served as deputy prime minister when these policies were implemented.

There were only two primary areas where a difference was noted between BN and PR. First, while both coalitions agreed to continue with affirmative action, PR argued that the policy had to be based on class, not race, targeting all Malaysians living in poverty. Second, there had been a discernible reduction in corruption in state governments led by PR. When PR and BN released their election manifestos, they were so markedly similar that each coalition would argue that its rival's policies on offer were originally conceived by it. The fact remained that these policies were being questioned by the electorate, both the rural poor and the urban middle class. This suggests that PR was devoid of fresh policy initiatives, a criticism lodged by business groups and NGOs. Crucially, too, PR could not counter Najib's new policy initiative of cash transfers to the poor, and its pledge of further handouts if returned to power. Called BRIM (*Bantuan Rakyat 1Malaysia*, or 1Malaysia People's Aid), this payout of RM4.6 billion reached seven million citizens, a factor that drew to BN the support of the poor across ethnic lines, including minority Indians whose votes could swing marginal seats either way.

PR also failed to win the election because, from a governance perspective, PAS's leadership of Kedah had been extremely contentious, being racked by party factionalism and the implementation of Islamic rules that were seen to be reactionary and divisive. In this under-developed state, the electorate's primary concern was policies to alleviate poverty, an issue PAS had not addressed. Another reason for PR's inability to win federal power was PAS's insistence on its plan to implement *hudud* law and an Islamic state, an argument that did not go down well with the electorate in the Borneo states and in southern states of the peninsula.

Conclusion

Even though UMNO has faced growing discontent over its manner of rule since the 1990s, there are two reasons why the opposition has not managed to secure power. First, the UMNO-led government has responded with relevant policies to check growing discontent, a core factor for BN's phenomenal victories in 1995 and 2004. Second, UMNO's persistent dominance is due to the nature of opposition coalitions that have been formed since 1990. These coalitions have comprised UMNO factions that have left the party, following their marginalisation from access to state rents, and formed pacts with other parties to mount strong challenges to unseat the BN. But the ex-UMNO elites have failed to convince the electorate that they now represent real change.

Malaysian society has consistently sent a message to all parties of the need to dispense with race- and religion-based politics. The government's promotion of concepts such as *Bangsa Malaysia* and *1Malaysia* reflects its awareness of the importance of espousing a trans-ethnic national identity. But past and present UMNO presidents must contend with the call of members for *ketuanan Melayu*, or Malay supremacy. UMNO's racialised discourse suggests a party caught in a time warp, while society has moved on. The religious-based PAS is confronted with a similar problem. Racialised and religious political discourses remain key features of both PR and BN, inhibiting constructive dialogue between member parties, and suggesting the existence of two dysfunctional coalitions. This partly explains the calls in civil society for the need to establish a 'third force'.

Since UMNO still enjoys support in the Malay heartland, while rapidly losing backing in the rest of the peninsula, the party is unlikely to dispense with unproductive race- and patronage-based policies. Abdullah and Najib both struggled to find a balance between serving public interests and pacifying UMNO factions through a fair distribution of state-generated rents. With mounting civil protests over conflict-of-interest situations, there is growing pressure on the government to introduce institutional reforms involving the devolution of power, but this is unlikely to happen in view of the executive's inability to check debilitating forms of party patronage and the serious possibility that power devolution could lead to UMNO's fall.

Two issues are evident about the state of politics and society. First, despite regular changes in the premiership after fractious UMNO feuds that undermined its electoral support, crony-based patronage continues to define its politics. UMNO factionalism, signifying considerable elite differentiation within the party, indicates the existence of several locations of power at the federal and state levels. UMNO's patron–client ties are not as asymmetrical as they once were, as a result of an appreciable decline in personalised politics, and factional leaders now have some leverage to undermine the capacity of party presidents to act unilaterally. UMNO members, for instance, openly criticised Abdullah and Najib when they channelled lucrative rents to their business allies.

Second, electoral trends indicate that Malaysian society has persisted in punishing parties articulating race- and religion-based politics. This suggests that UMNO's position is precarious in the long term, particularly if it cannot sustain rural Malay support, which in 1990, 1999 and 2008 had swung to the opposition. Electoral trends further indicate that attempts to consolidate power will not augur well for political elites. Public criticisms as well as huge demonstrations in urban areas led by the middle class in 1999, in 2008 and in the period leading up to and in the immediate aftermath of the 2013 elections indicate an electorate intolerant of power concentration and abuse. For this middle class, it is insufficient that UMNO ensures economic growth to justify retaining power. UMNO is aware that for things to remain the same, the government must institute reforms to devolve power and check patronage.[30] However, UMNO has persistently refused to alter a patronage system that allows it to feed off policies to enrich its members, and it is unlikely to do so unless it loses power.

5

The Workers' Party of Brazil: The pragmatic trap

Guilherme Simões Reis

Brazil has had two consecutive left-wing presidents representing the Workers' Party (PT, Partido dos Trabalhadores): Luiz Inácio Lula da Silva, who held office for two terms, and currently Dilma Rousseff, the favourite in the polls for the elections that will be held in October 2014. The PT's accession to power was part of a leftist wave in South America, which saw the left win elections in all countries but Colombia. At the same time, Brazil, together with Uruguay, differs from the other countries in the region in that it has a strong and institutionalised left-wing political party that has been active for decades, having taken part in all elections since it was founded in 1980.

What does it mean to have a left-wing party governing a developing country with serious historical, social and economic problems? There are many different constraints on a socialist party in government: the balance of forces inside parliament, the interests and preferences of the conservative majority of voters, right-wing control of the media, the economic structure and so on. On the other hand, if socialism is to represent more than an empty category, a socialist party must not only pursue gradual and cumulative reform in the face of such obstacles, but also try to overcome such constraints in order to make possible greater advances in the future.

Besides these external constraints, there are also internal ones, which are of greater interest here. In the real world, parties are not unitary actors, but consist of groups of people with different interests, preferences, views, goals, interpretations of challenges and strategies. In order to simplify that complexity and make analysis feasible, we can divide democratic socialist parties into two broad groups:[1] a 'purist' faction, which avoids coalitions and refuses to deviate from the ideal party programme, and a 'pragmatic' faction, which acknowledges the need for coalition-building, as the party does not have the support of the majority of voters, but which in the process may lose the focus on long-term goals, by concentrating on day-to-day politics.

If one of these two groups becomes dominant and stronger than the other, the party as a whole will lose its 'social democratic character', turning itself either into a 'ghetto' party – that is, one having a narrow constituency and no real chance of impacting on national policies – or a non-ideological office-seeking party – one that does not offer anything different from the conservative parties and that abandons radical social and economic changes.

The Workers' Party of Brazil is not safe from the second risk. Indeed, there has been a trend in its history to turn itself into a pragmatic office-seeking party. Winning presidential elections has become the most important goal in the view of most party leaders, and the original concerns about changing society and weakening conservative forces in national politics, both in state-level governments and in the Congress, have been neglected. This trend is directly linked to the balance of forces in the party: the pragmatists have become, from one presidential term to the next, stronger and stronger, a situation aggravated as outsiders enter the PT, attracted by its position as the main party in government.[2]

This does not mean that PT governments are the same as previous conservative ones, or that they are not making changes in people's lives. In many respects the Lula and Rousseff governments are the most left-leaning governments the country has ever had, but there is no longer a major concern about making deeper changes. In its opposition to neoliberalism, the PT defends state intervention in economy and large investments in social policies of providing public services and redistributing income. Still, several scholars[3] hold that the party has undergone an ideological moderation over time, following a Przeworskian path[4] similar to the one traversed by socialist parties in Western Europe in the first half of 20th century. Indeed, nowadays the party is in regular dialogue with businessmen and implements strict fiscal policies.

The growth of the Workers' Party

The PT was formed in 1980 during a period of political opening which saw the legalisation of multi-party politics. It came about through the association of various left-wing groups, trade unionists included, and acquired the character of a 'factions party' (*partido de tendências*, as it is called in Brazil). It grew continuously without interruptions, initially in opposition to the dictatorship then ruling Brazil. It was concerned, therefore, not only to advocate social fairness, but also to promote political and civil rights.

There were three individuals involved in initial discussions about the foundation of a workers' party, the so-called 'historical union leaders': Lula himself, then president of the union of metal workers; Olívio Dutra, president of the union of bank employees; and Jacó Bittar, president of the union of oil workers – all three based in São Paulo state. The party's foundation was given impetus by strikes in the motor industry in 1978 in the state of São Paulo.[5]

Besides trade unionists, the party also secured the adherence of other groups, such as student and middle-class Marxist organisations; progressive movements within the Catholic Church influenced by liberation theology; the intelligentsia based in universities and research institutes; peasant and landless workers' organisations; and some politicians from the opposition party to the military dictatorship, the Brazilian Democratic Movement (MDB).[6]

From the outset the PT was critical of other 'progressive' movements and organisations, such as the MDB, the populist Brazilian Labour Party (PTB) and the historical Brazilian Communist Party (PCB). The MDB, for instance, was dismissed as being heterogeneous and made up of elite cadres, incapable of fighting for workers' political independence.[7]

The founders of the PT set themselves in opposition not only to the authoritarian regime, but also to the period of democratic government in Brazil between 1945 and 1964, which it criticised as a 'formal and parliamentarian democracy, the product of a deal made among dominant elites', excluding 'organised popular participation'. The PT has always considered itself as marking a deep change in the Brazilian polity, as is clear from Lula's speech as party president at its first national convention:

> The Workers' Party is a historical innovation in this country. It is an innovation not only in political life but also in the history of the left. It is a party that was born boosted by mass movements and people's struggles throughout Brazil. It is a party that was born from the understanding that the workers developed after being manoeuvred by bourgeois politicians for decades and after listening to rigmarole from purportedly working-class vanguard parties. Only workers may conquer what they have the right to. Nobody has ever gifted us; nobody will ever give us anything for free.[8]

After Lula nearly won the 1989 presidential elections, the right and centre parties saw the need to join together, despite their differences, in a single bloc, so as to keep the PT out of power. Consequently, from the 1990s onwards the PT has influenced the behaviour of all other political players in Brazil: 'Petism' and 'Anti-Petism' help to mobilise a great majority of the voters, as Singer points out. One can say that the PT has caused a realignment in Brazilian politics, which have been split between those who support the party and those who oppose it.

As the PT was initially built out of many different groups opposed to the military regime, it emerged almost as a front, unlike previous leftist parties in Brazil. This diversity has been a mark of the party's organisational development, and since its foundation it has been characterised by divisions and ideological differences between the component groups.

PT achieved electoral growth by putting forward its own candidacies in majoritarian elections (for the presidency, for state governorships, mayoralties and senatorships) and refusing to enter coalitions with other parties, emphasising itself as a new force in politics and claiming to represent a unique *Petista* way of governing.[9] This strategy worked well: gradually PT grew and imposed itself as the major force within the left, overcoming the communists from PCB and the Communist Party of Brazil (PC do B) and, later, the Democratic Labour Party (PDT), heir of the old Brazilian Labour Party. In the 1989 presidential elections, Leonel Brizola, leader of the PDT, led the polls for some time, but in the end he finished in third place.

There was a slowdown in the party's electoral growth in the 1992 local elections (unsurprisingly, internal reforms took place in the years following). But the party won in four state capitals – Porto Alegre, Belo Horizonte, Goiânia and Rio Branco – and only lost in the runoff in São Paulo, Rio de Janeiro and João Pessoa. As a result of the elections the PT ceased to be a 'party from São Paulo state'. The PT elected the mayors of 53 towns throughout the country, the highest number in its history until then, although the number of people ruled by the PT declined, as it lost in the biggest Brazilian city, São Paulo.

In 1994 Lula lost the presidential election to Fernando Henrique Cardoso, from the liberal Party of Brazilian Social Democracy (PSDB), who was boosted by the popularity of his economic Plan Real (to deal with hyper-inflation), despite a poll of a few months previously which predicted that 40 per cent of the votes would go to the PT's candidate. Although defeated, Lula won five million votes more than in 1989. In addition, the PT elected state governors for the first time, in Espírito Santo and Federal District, as well as four new senators.

In the 1996 local elections the PT kept advancing in the countryside. The proportion of the population ruled by the party decreased once more, but the number of towns ruled by the PT increased to 115 in all the states with the exception of four. It was also the party whose candidates participated in the run-off in most state capitals (although it lost on five occasions and won only in Belem and Porto Alegre).

Lula suffered his third presidential defeat in 1998, when Brizola offered to run as candidate for the vice-presidency. Though the PT increased its representation by only nine seats in its bloc in the Chamber of Deputies, the lower chamber of Congress, it was now by far the strongest force on the left, which had only a third of the seats. More importantly, in the 2000 local elections, the PT became the party with the most votes in Brazil, electing mayors in 187 towns. In 2002, besides finally electing Lula as president, the PT became, for the first time, the largest party in the Chamber of Deputies. If one calculates the figures after the 'traditional' moves of representatives to different parties post-election, the PT had a total of 93 federal deputies, or 18.1 per cent of the house.

Internal struggle

The PT has always suffered from internal conflicts between its numerous factions. Since the beginning, more or less radical forces coexisted inside the party, Trotskyist or Leninist in orientation, many of them entering the party from armed struggle against the military regime. According to Secco, the importance of these radical groups – which made up just ten per cent of party members – was limited to their theoretical and ideological contribution, as they did not impact significantly on social movements or elections.[10] But their presence did contribute to strengthening the radicalism of the party's discourse.

The PT's failure in the 1982 elections favoured anti-institutional pressures from the revolutionary wing.[11] Moderates such as Lula and other union leaders reacted by creating the group called Articulation in 1983 to give expression to the views of the independents.[12] For most of its history this group has led the party and has beaten the left wing in internal elections, with the exception of a short period in the first half of the 1990s when the 'PT's left' took control of the party. As Sarti states,[13] Articulation promoted the centralisation of decision-making, contrary to the original idea of building the PT as a decentralised party with a bottom-up organisation centred on groups, factions and autonomous regional committees. The initial intention of reaching internal decisions by direct democracy and in local and issue-based small groups was abandoned and the party became bureaucratised, with professional leaders taking charge of coordinating the party.[14]

Articulation never accepted quietly the resistance of the more leftist sections to its leadership, accusing them of a 'two-colour activism' (*militância de duas camisas*), that is, of working as a faction inside the party, not accepting majority decisions and instead promoting their own views. Indeed, internal decisions taken by the party have been mostly the ones proposed by Articulation. This majority sector also saw itself 'as a popular reaction to the party left's elitism and vanguardism', merging a vague idea of socialism with a pragmatic focus on day-to-day political struggles.[15]

In 1989, when the leftist and clandestine Revolutionary Communist Party (PRC) ceased to exist after the fall of the Berlin Wall, most of its members merged with part of another minor faction to form a new group, this time on the 'PT's right wing', called Radical Democracy, led by the ex-guerrilla José Genoino. It was then that Articulation became for the first time the force in the centre of the party, oscillating both left and right.[16]

Although small, the Marxist groups had more centralised and better structured organisation than the centrist factions, making it possible for them to punch above their weight in the party. In reaction, the moderate majority, in an effort to exert a monopoly of party control, did not allow proportional representation in internal elections to the committee until 1989, and did not allow internal rules that would have made it possible for the rank and file to control the party's legislative representatives and office-holders, as those leaders came mostly from the moderate group.[17]

According to Sarti,[18] Articulation's dominance was maintained as well by a 'regional centralisation', as the party's organisational growth took place by expansion from its centre in São Paulo. This has ensured that cadres from that state form the majority of the party's national leaders, particularly those from Articulation and Radical Democracy, the most moderate groups inside the PT. The strategy of always having their own candidate was strictly applied only in national elections or elections for office in São Paulo; in other regions it was relaxed to facilitate trade-offs with other parties to secure national and São Paulo state offices.

The deepening of internal division and of the contradictions inside Articulation caused a split in this majority group. Some of their leaders created the Left Articulation and together with Socialist Democracy and some smaller groups beat the most right-wing sectors for control of the PT for the first (and last) time. In 1995, Articulation – Unity in Struggle (the most moderate part of old Articulation) merged with Radical Democracy to form the Majority Sector, regaining party control from the radical groups. One of the most important leaders of Majority Sector, José Dirceu, became president of the party with the role of professionalising it, and he played a central and pragmatic role in its electoral expansion and in coalition-building.

In 2003 four legislators from different leftist sectors were expelled from the PT for criticising the government and voting against social security reform, which sought to change the retirement rules of public servants, a historical constituency of the party. One year later, the four were among the founders of Party Socialism and Freedom (PSOL), which attracted a significant number of former PT members. This split had a moderate electoral and trade union impact but it proved significant in changing the PT's internal balance of forces. As many of the most leftist members left to join PSOL, the pragmatic wing of the PT became even more dominant. From then on, internal disputes have become more personality-based than before.

In the first Lula government, which implemented an austere economic policy, critical voices in PT were silenced not only by the threat of sanctions, but also by co-option using a carrot-and-stick approach. Following a path of 'coalition presidentialism', Lula took into account not only partisan and regional factors in choosing his ministers, but also looked for cadres who would represent all the different sectors within his own party.

The government confronted a serious crisis in 2005, when the scandal known as 'Mensalão' broke. Critics alleged that the government had made payments to deputies to have its projects approved, while defenders contested that version explaining that the scandal was only a matter of the irregular financing of election campaigns, which, though not allowed, is widespread. As a result of the crisis, some members of Majority Sector joined Socialist Democracy to build a new broad movement called Message to the Party, while the majority of the Majority Sector changed their name to Building a New Brazil (CNB) in 2007.

Internal debates were fierce until 2005, with the radical sectors claiming the kudos for programmatic changes, such as the implementation of a participatory budget, a popular policy implemented by the PT in state-level and local-level governments but ignored by the president. As Lula's government moved to the left and the opposition tried to take advantage of the Mensalão scandal, the various groups inside PT muted their criticism and preferred instead to defend the government's achievements.[19] The leadership of Lula was of extreme importance in keeping the party united in the middle of crisis, but that does not mean that the most symbolic cadre of PT is neutral: Lula is the most popular of the pragmatists.

The pragmatic dominance

The risk to the PT of losing its ideological identity has grown as the dominance of the pragmatists increases and the purists are weakened. According to Secco, 77 per cent of PT members have joined the party since 2001 (one year before Lula's victory), many attracted by the possibility of access to office. Becoming less left-wing and more concerned with office-seeking, the PT has grown more and more like its biggest partner in Rousseff's government, the PMDB, a phenomenon that may be called the 'Peemedebisation' of the PT.

At the same time, the party PSOL has developed a role of unconstructive opposition, tending to oppose everything that is supported by the government, and very often building ad hoc parliamentary coalitions together with the right-wing parties PSDB and

Democrats (DEM), besides attacking all PT's presidential candidacies while staying relatively indifferent to the PSDB's candidates. In all this, PSOL does not offer a real alternative to the left, or function as a stick to stop the Peemedebisation of PT and its office-seeking trend.

The only possible way of avoiding becoming a purely office-seeking party such as PMDB is to strengthen the purist barrier to pragmatist advancement. This could happen as a result of external pressure, if PSOL took a more constructive and less 'ghetto party' role, or by internal pressure, which would be the better option for PT members, if the radical groups and the Message to the Party broad sector were strengthened vis-à-vis Building a New Brazil (CNB). Such a realignment could be assisted by the return of internal discussions about policy programmes, which are almost nonexistent nowadays owing to the routine of day-to-day public management.

The strength of pragmatism inside PT is also related to its funding. Historically the party has been financed mostly by the public party fund (which all the parties inside parliament share) and by its office-holders: 30 per cent of their earnings must be given to the party.[20] Most of the PT's legislators are from CNB. The majority of the members who attend the party's meetings are advisers or have other political jobs (and few are voluntary activists), which means that they are politically and financially dependent on the mostly pragmatic party leaders: the party bureaucracy is increasingly becoming the preserve of office-holders.[21] These characteristics have prompted Ribeiro[22] to consider the PT as a cartel party, following Katz and Mair's approach.[23] What is more, the party increased its campaign funding since 2002 with contributions from private firms,[24] and in return its candidates satisfy interests that are at variance with left-wing goals.

In 2001 the PT instituted a supposedly democratic way of selecting its leaders: the process of direct election (PED), in which all the party members can vote. Since then, however, the pragmatists have become stronger and the internal balance of forces even more uneven. As Secco states, the PED is susceptible to the abuse of economic power.[25] The groups able to attract the greatest funding for their intra-party campaigns

■ Table 1: Party fragmentation in South America and size of president's party (Lower Chamber, 1989–2002)

Countries	Effective number of parties*			President's party (%)		
	Average	Minimum	Maximum	Average	Minimum	Maximum
Brazil	8.1	7.1	8.7	16	5	21
Argentina	3.1	2.8	3.4	44	33	52
Bolivia	4.6	3.9	5.4	29	25	40
Chile	5.7	4.7	7.1	26	12	32
Colombia	3.5	2.2	6.5	35	13	60
Ecuador	6.2	5.1	7.4	20	4	43
Peru	4.2	2.9	5.8	31	3	56
Uruguay	3.6	3.1	4.3	35	32	39
Venezuela	4.3	2.8	5.5	28	13	48

Note: The effective number of parties (ENP) is an index of party fragmentation created by Laakso and Taagapera in 1979, taking into account both their number and their relative size.
Source: F. Anastasia, C.R. Melo and F. Santos, *Governabilidade e Representação Política na América do Sul* (Rio de Janeiro and São Paulo, 2004)

are those that support policies and a way of formulating them which are the furthest removed from those that animated the creation of the PT.

The dominance of pragmatists in the PT is also suited to the balance of forces among the parties in the country. The Brazilian party system is very fragmented. Although the PT has consolidated itself as one of the two biggest parliamentary parties (together with the PMDB), it has never won as much as a quarter of the seats in Congress. A single-party majority government is unimaginable in Brazil. The country has always had coalition governments in its democratic history. As Table 1 shows, party systems in the other South American countries are much less fragmented and the parties of all Brazilian presidents have never secured a majority. Moreover, left-wing allies have had a relatively small number of deputies, which has compelled the government to include conservative parties in the ruling coalition, particularly the PMDB, and this has reduced the chance of major reforms in policy.

Table 2, even though it does not include Lula's second government

Table 2: Parties in presidential coalitions in Brazil between 1985 and 2007

President	Period	Parties in coalition
José Sarney	03/1985 to 02/1986	PMDB, PFL, PTB, PDS
	02/1986 to 03/1990	PMDB, PFL
Fernando Collor	03/1990 to 10/1990	PMDB, PFL, PRN
	10/1990 to 01/1992	PFL, PDS, PRN
	01/1992 to 04/1992	PFL, PDS
	04/1992 to 10/1992	PFL, PDS, PSDB, PTB, PL
Itamar Franco	10/1992 to 01/1993	PMDB, PFL, PSDB, PTB, PDT, PSB
	01/1993 to 05/1993	PMDB, PFL, PSDB, PTB, PDT, PSB, PT
	05/1993 to 09/1993	PMDB, PFL, PSDB, PTB, PSB
	09/1993 to 01/1994	PMDB, PFL, PSDB, PTB, PP
	01/1994 to 01/1995	PMDB, PFL, PSDB, PP
F.H. Cardoso (I)	01/1995 to 04/1996	PSDB, PMDB, PFL, PTB
	04/1996 to 12/1998	PSDB, PFL, PMDB, PTB, PPB, PPS
F.H. Cardoso (II)	01/1996 to 03/2002	PSDB, PFL, PMDB, PPB
	03/2002 to 12/2002	PSDB, PMDB, PPB
Lula da Silva (I)	01/2003 to 01/2004	PT, PL, PCdoB, PSB, PTB, PDT, PPS, PV
	01/2004 to 01/2005	PT, PL, PCdoB, PSB, PTB, PPS, PV, PMDB
	02/2005 to 05/2005	PT, PL, PCdoB, PSB, PTB, PV, PMDB
	05/2005 to 07/2005	PT, PL, PCdoB, PSB, PTB, PMDB
	07/2005 to 01/2007	PT, PL, PCdoB, PSB, PTB, PP, PMDB

Sources: For the governments led by Sarney, Collor, Franco and the first by Cardoso: O. Amorim Neto, *Presidencialismo e Governabilidade nas Américas* (Rio de Janeiro, 2006). For both Cardoso's governments and the first of Lula's: A.C. Figueiredo, 'Instabilidade política no primeiro governo Lula: Conflito partidário, ideologia e instituições' in M.R.S. Lima (ed.), *Desempenho de Governos Progressistas no Cone Sul: Agendas Alternativas ao Neoliberalismo* (Rio de Janeiro, 2008), 47–65.

nor Rousseff's, shows that all governments in Brazil since the end of the military dictatorship have been coalitions, most of them involving more than three parties. In addition, the first Lula government had a particularly high number of parties: between six and eight.

Since the PT's national hegemony in the left-of-centre of the political system has been assured, the party's priority has become to win the presidential elections (as well as state-level city mayoral elections in São Paulo, which is by far the most populous state and the financial centre of the country and from which most of party's leaders come). There is very little concern about the policies implemented by allied regional and local governments (excluding São Paulo) and about strengthening the PT's politicians there. Because of this and because the PT does not intend to threaten its conservative allies, there is no serious move to change the constraints imposed by the balance of forces in Congress: no stronger campaign to increase the party's share of seats, no change to the electoral system.[26]

Consequently, despite its electoral achievements and its positive successes in reducing poverty and unemployment, the PT has not overcome the challenge of attracting voters to the left and thereby making possible a socialist hegemony. Instead, it has simply moved to the centre of the ideological spectrum in order to win the support of the median voter.

The priority given to winning presidential elections relegates to a lesser importance any concern to increase the number of deputies from the party or the number of governors and mayors, thereby providing excessive space to its conservative allies, particularly the PMDB. It does not help to change dramatically the balance of forces. Instead, the PT is nowadays left with no alternative but building coalitions that represent serious constraints to any socialist advancement.

One example of this is the significant size within the government coalition of socially conservative factions, mostly linked to representatives of Pentecostal Christianity. Here one can mention the remarkable participation of the Brazilian Republican Party (PRB), which is basically the political arm of the Universal Church of the Kingdom of God (one of whose main leaders is the senator and bishop Marcelo Crivella, ex-gospel singer and nephew of Bishop Edir Macedo). This reliance on conservative forces makes it much more difficult to promote social and identity issues, such as homosexual marriage or abortion, than distributive issues, which have a better reception among these culturally conservative groups, which have mostly a lower-class constituency.

The balance of forces among parties also impacts on the way the government deals with agriculture. In Brazil, soya cultivation in large estates is favoured over more labour-intensive forms of agriculture. The members of parliament associated with agribusiness, spread through many different parties, are among the most conservative allies of the PT's government, although they had previously supported the PSDB government. As the PT wants to please both capital and labour, it does not challenge the lobbyists of land owners, or confront their anti-environmentalist actions and the recurrent slave labour accusations against them.

There are two different ministries in Brazilian government dealing with agrarian issues, with contradictory policies: one of them, the Ministry of Agrarian Development, is an ally of the Movement of Landless Workers (MST) and is controlled by the PT's left-wing faction Socialist Democracy (DS), while the other, the Ministry of Agriculture, is on the hands of the PMDB. Unsurprisingly, the former favours land reform and family agriculture, while the latter defends agribusiness interests. The Ministry of Labour also has a programme to support cooperative methods but between 2003 and 2009 only 250 000 families benefited, which means that, although well planned, it is not a priority in the government's budget.

Conclusion

The social progress achieved by the PT during its three terms in presidential government is significant and has brought about a change in trend in South American politics. This has not happened, however, without obstacles and contradictions.

Brazil is internationally regarded as a regional leader and power, member of BRICS and player of a prominent role among developing nations. This is what is expected of a country with a huge internal market, a broad range of various natural resources and a diversified industrial sector. These features also point to its relatively significant ability to develop autonomous policies, which – in the hands of a left-wing party – could advance economic and civil rights. As Singer states,[27] even the great number of unemployed workers has engaged in the electoral process, even though without proper ideological direction.

The constraints on the scope of party politics are serious, and more difficult to manage than in neighbouring countries. Outside the PT, the balance of forces is also adverse, as the party system is fragmented and potential left-wing allies are feeble. As we have discussed, one of the greatest difficulties lies inside the party: pragmatism reigns supreme.

Brazil's presidential system is thus biased in favour of the conservative pragmatists, who happily agree to be part of a government coalition in order to gain access to office and power. The party believes it has no alternative but to attract to the government groups linked to the elite, the financial sector, agribusiness and religious conservatism. With winning presidential elections having become the only non-negotiable goal, there is no serious effort to change the balance of forces that over-represents the conservatives and keeps the left feeble.

Until now, it has been possible for the PT in government to favour both the traditional constituency of a left party and the economic elite. This cannot continue forever. When the crisis comes, the party will need to choose between labour and capital. At that stage, unless the purist groups within the party are strengthened and the Peemedebisation process stops, there is little chance of the socialist alternative emerging as victor.

6

Information and communications technology and the transformation of the Chinese Communist Party

Ping Shum and Zheng Yongnian

With more than 85 million members, the Chinese Communist Party (CCP) is the largest political party in the world and the ruling party of the most populated country of the world. The CCP is not a political party as the term is understood in the West. Effectively the only ruling party of the People's Republic of China (PRC) since 1949, the CCP has become an institution of the state, controlling the government, the military and the media. It was the CCP that established the PRC and is, therefore, the 'property rights' owner of the country. The relationship between the CCP and the state is similar to the traditional relationship between the emperor and his premier. As the party 'owns' the PRC, the government, led by the premier, can be considered the administrator of the state. In fact, one can argue that the party is the first layer of administration, and the state the second. Nearly all government officials are party members, especially at senior level. The top official of a province, city or county is the party secretary rather than the governor or mayor. Many of the state and CCP agencies are intertwined: for instance, the State Council Information Office and the CCP's External Propaganda Office are the same institution but with different names. To a large extent, the absolute authority of the CCP over the country is unparalleled in the rest of the world.

The advent of new information and communications technology (ICT) has brought both challenges and opportunities to the CCP. Nearly half of the population are Internet users, and among them 75 per cent have access to the Internet via mobile phone. Public opinion formulated online has increasingly had an impact on the party-state and led to policy changes on some occasions. With the advent of the Internet the once-powerful Propaganda Department is no longer able to exercise total control over the flow of information. Facing this new environment, the CCP has not only attempted to reinforce its censorship mechanisms but also introduced innovative propaganda strategies in order to maintain its domination over the state and society.

We argue in this chapter that the CCP has transformed itself in line with ICT developments while keeping unchanged the structure of party domination. This chapter will first give a brief account of Internet development in China and the impact of Internet public opinion on the state and society. It will then look at the ways that the CCP has adapted itself in order to stay in power, by analysing relations between party and society and between party and government. At the party–society level, we will examine how the Internet has empowered the CCP to dominate society while strengthening itself in delivering services to the public. At the party–government level, we will examine how the Internet has empowered the party to control the government and promote better governance.

Internet development in China

China's Internet users increased from 620 000 in 1997 to more than 600 million by the end of 2013.[1] It surpassed the United States in 2008 as the largest country in terms of its netizen population. Despite tight control from the Propaganda Department of the CCP on the flow of information and strict regulation by the government, the Internet in China has grown at a remarkable pace. As of December 2012, China had 2.68 million websites, with the majority registered as commercial.[2]

The Internet has brought many unprecedented challenges to the party-state. In 2010 there were 180 000 protests, strikes and other mass disturbances in China. Some of them were organised with the aid of the Internet, through blogs, email, online forums and Weibo (a Chinese word for microblogging). Public opinion formulated in cyberspace has translated into public pressure and, on many occasions, brought down corrupt officials or forced the party-state to adjust its policies. Compared with traditional media, the Internet in China enjoys relatively few controls from the Propaganda Department and is often driven by commercial interests. At the same time, the unique nature of information flow on the Internet – which is instant, interactive and boundless – has undermined the effectiveness of traditional methods of propaganda.

Public opinion formulated through social media can be considered a social force that poses challenges to the domination of the CCP. As ICT evolves, new social media platforms operated by commercial companies in China have emerged. One of the fastest-growing social media platforms is Weibo, which is reported to have reached half a billion users by the end of 2012.[3] Its potential for generating or influencing online public opinion is becoming increasingly clear. Studies suggest that more than 73 per cent of Weibo users consider it as their main source of news information; at the same time, expressing thoughts and opinions by tweeting is the most common activity among Weibo users, accounting for 74.3 per cent of use.[4] As with Twitter, a Weibo user can post any statement or comment without prior approval from the party-state. A tweet on Weibo can be forwarded by followers within seconds and reach tens of thousands of people before it is detected and deleted.

One of the ways in which the Internet plays a role in reducing corruption is by providing a platform for the public to expose official wrongdoing. Similar to the development of online public opinion originating on online forums and chat rooms, Weibo is increasingly becoming an important media platform that is not under the direct control of the Propaganda Department. By the first half of 2011, Weibo had surpassed online forums to become the second most important originator of news about public incidents, after traditional news media, with 18 per cent of the most discussed 'hot' issues being exposed by Weibo users.[5]

As corruption among party and state officials has become widespread, exposés by netizens is more and more common. Although there are many official channels to report corruption, such as the 'Netizen Interaction' column on the website of the National Bureau of Corruption Prevention, non-official channels, such as Weibo, seem to be preferred by netizens. The director of Internet public opinion monitoring office of People's Daily Online, Zhu Xinhua, acknowledged that the Internet has become a platform for different interest groups, and disadvantaged groups in particular, to express their opinion.[6]

Netizens in China have taken full advantage of ICT in exposing CCP officials' corrupt behaviour. On many occasions, public participation has led to the arrest and prosecution of officials engaged in corrupt activities. One such case emerged in 2008, when a photo of a local official in Nanjing smoking extravagant cigarettes well beyond the reach of his salary was posted on a popular online forum in China. He was further exposed by other netizens for allegedly wearing a luxury watch and driving an expensive car. The official concerned was later dismissed and sentenced to 11 years in jail.

In a more recent case, in December 2012, Luo Changping, a prominent investigative journalist in China, accused Liu Tienan, deputy head of the National Development and Reform Commission, of participating in questionable financial deals, fabricating his academic record, and threatening to murder his former mistress. These revelations were posted on Luo Changping's Weibo page. Liu was consequently dismissed from his position in August 2013 and investigated.

In the 12 months after Xi Jinping took over as head of the CCP in November 2012, 88 officials at the provincial and municipal levels were investigated for alleged wrongdoing, with 18 among them exposed via the Internet.[7] The potential of influencing state policy via Internet and online public opinion is becoming more apparent, not only in China but also in other authoritarian regimes.

Social media, such as Facebook, Twitter and YouTube, are said to have played an important role in facilitating Iran's mass protests in 2009 as well as the Arab Spring across North Africa and the Middle East from December 2010 on.[8] In much the same way, a number of small-scale public gatherings, mobilised via social media, took place in over a dozen cities in China from February 2011 on. This so-called 'Jasmine Revolution' failed to take root and was quickly suppressed by the Chinese government.[9] Although Western-based social media are banned in China, the country has its own equivalents, such as RenRen, Weibo and Youku, which have proved to be extremely popular among Chinese netizens. The potential power of the Internet to challenge and even overthrow a regime has become obvious.

Literature on China's Internet

As the Internet is often considered a liberating and democratising force, a number of scholars have examined the impact of the Internet on China's civil society and its implication for the development of democracy in the country. Supported by several high-profile cases in 2003 and 2004, Tai demonstrated how China's Internet users have exerted pressure on the party-state to change its actions and policies in deference to public demands. He concluded from this that the Internet democratises the communication of information in Chinese society, and allows netizens to engage in public debates on social and political issues.[10]

Yang's study has focused on online activism, which he breaks into two types: struggles for recognition and against discrimination, and struggles against oppression and exploitation. He argues that 'power seeks domination, it incurs resistance' and 'the forms of online activism respond to the forms of control'.[11] In his view, with the further development of online activism, people's aspirations for basic citizenship rights will be mobilised; and he is optimistic that these civic engagements in 'unofficial democracy' may lead to full democracy in China.

Studying the impact of the Internet on Chinese state and civil society, Zheng observed that the party-state controls the Internet and uses it to mobilise social support for its causes. However, he did also point to several cases where online public opinion led to policy changes by the party-state: 'the interaction between state and society over Internet-based public space has transformed both actors and provided the dynamics for political changes in China. Zheng persuasively argues that the Internet empowers both state and society, as collective actions originating on the Internet help in promoting political openness, which, in turn, makes the regime become more accountable to its citizens.[12]

Most of the current literature on China's Internet policies focuses on traditional and passive methods of blocking, filtering and censorship. Two Western-based Internet research projects on China, 'Internet Filtering in China' and the 'Berkeley China Internet Project', have both emphasised the Internet control methods implemented by the Chinese party-state.[13] But few studies have fully examined how the party-state makes positive use of ICT. Shambaugh, as well as Chase and Mulvenon, points out that the CCP employs proactive efforts on the Internet in order to consolidate its power, but they stop short of exploring how exactly the party-state uses the Internet to engage in proactive propaganda.[14] Zhou acknowledges that whereas information in Chinese society has been subject to strict control, the CCP has also taken proactive steps to control the Internet, but he only uses *Qiangguo Luntan* (Strengthening China Forum), a popular online forum of the CCP's mouthpiece, the *People's Daily*, as a case study to demonstrate the proactive policy implemented by the party-state.[15] Since Zhou's study was published in 2006, there have been a number of other, more sophisticated proactive strategies employed by the party-state, such as the promotion of e-government and the setting up of Weibo accounts by government institutions and individuals.

Transformation: Adapt and change

Although facing numerous challenges, the Chinese government has been able to enhance the state's capacity to govern effectively by means of institutional adaptations and policy adjustments, displaying what Nathan terms 'authoritarian resilience'.[16] The development of ICT has compelled the Chinese party-state to transform itself in order to maintain domination over the state and society. The media forms one of the factors in stabilising authoritarian regimes, and the CCP's adaptation and change of strategy towards the Internet has contributed to the Chinese regime's survival.

Instead of remaining reactive, the CCP has become proactive by introducing various strategies to exert its domination over both the state and society and thus maintain its ascendancy over these actors.[17] With the expansion of ICT and a growing netizen population in China, a new form of public opinion is taking shape in the virtual world of the Internet, which has started to influence government policy-making. In the first national propaganda work conference held by Hu Jintao after his appointment as general secretary of the CCP in 2002, he urged party propaganda officials to improve their work on the new media and push forward an initiative to guide public opinion.[18]

A decision of the CCP Central Committee 'on strengthening the party's ruling ability' adopted in September 2004 pointed out that '[the party's] ability to guide public opinion has to be improved, the Internet's development and supervision urgently needs to be reinforced and reformed'.[19] This decision urged that 'positive public opinion' be cultivated on the Internet, indicating the government's use of the Internet not only to consolidate its control of society but also to enhance its legitimacy.[20] This is regarded as the first important document concerning Internet propaganda policy openly published by the CCP Central Committee.[21] In January 2007 the CCP Politburo held a seminar to study the development of Internet technology worldwide, as well as the construction and regulation of China's Internet culture.[22] During the seminar, Hu, the general secretary, urged party officials at all levels to enhance their knowledge of the Internet; and recommended that party and government departments at all levels should take measures to guide public opinion and develop government websites.[23] The CCP Central Committee released a document soon after the seminar, which has become the guideline for and framework of Internet propaganda policy.[24] As Weibo became increasingly popular, the party-state extended its attention to social media. In October 2011 the CCP Central Committee issued another document reiterating the importance of guiding online public opinion, particularly in respect of social media.[25]

Transformation of party–society relations

China has achieved unprecedented rapid transformation since the introduction of reform policy in the late 1970s by Deng Xiaoping. Facing drastic socio-economic changes and an increasingly complex society, the party has tried to perfect its governing machine by maintaining its Leninist structure, on the one hand, and adapting to changing conditions, on the other.[26] At the same time as introducing modern state institutions and incorporating democratic elements, such as direct village elections, ICT provides a new tool for the party to achieve its goals. The Internet has empowered the CCP to dominate society while strengthening itself in delivering services to the public. The head of the Ministry for Information Industry commented that the control of information and lending credibility to the image of the leadership are important tasks for e-government.[27] One of the main functions of the Government Online Project Service Centre, which was established in 1998, is to act as a 'propaganda centre', to publicise events concerning projects organised by central and provincial governments.[28]

A study on e-government projects across the world has identified three major categories: e-governance, e-service and e-knowledge.[29] As Chinese governments at all levels of the state are by far the largest owners of information resources in the country,[30] the party-state is able to release information favourable to it by means of the promotion of e-knowledge. The vast majority of local governments have set up portals that enable citizens to contact the government via email. By the end of 2013, 97 per cent of departments at the central level, 100 per cent at provincial level and 98 per cent at the county level had set up official websites.[31]

The CCP's official newspaper, the *People's Daily*, set up a special website in 2006 to serve as online message boards for netizens to interact with party chiefs and heads of government at provincial, municipal and county level.[32] Netizens may leave comments, file complaints or make inquiries on officials' message boards. Messages posted online are mostly related to issues to do with daily life, such as environmental protection, land disputes and employment issues. The website received 1 300 to 1 500 new messages from netizens daily in 2010.[33] In the first 11 months of 2013, it helped in solving 70 000 issues raised by netizens, 43 per cent up compared with the previous year.[34] Surveys over a period of three to four years at the provincial level suggest that provinces that respond better to netizens' concerns posted on message boards saw a decrease in the number of petitions (i.e. fewer people filed complaints with the Bureau for Letters and Visits).[35]

One case known as the 'brother roar incident' demonstrated how the message board answered people's needs.[36] In 2010, a resident in Guangzhou, a major city in South China, went to the government's legal office on business. The official behind the desk not only refused to serve him without giving any reason but started to shout at him. The resident recorded the whole incident and posted the audio clip on the online message board of Guangzhou's mayor and quickly attracted attention from state media as well as the government. The official, who was labelled 'brother roar', was suspended temporarily and forced to apologise in public.

Realising the significance of Weibo in shaping people's attitudes to the government, the CCP has devoted much effort to this new media platform. Over 240 000 state institutions and individual officials set up accounts on Weibo by late 2013[37] in order to engage directly with netizens. Those setting up Weibo accounts included CCP committees, government departments, courts and prosecutors, as well as committees of the local People's Congress and political advisory bodies. More than 20 departments at the ministerial level have opened accounts at Sina Weibo, including Commerce, Culture, Foreign Affairs, Health and Public Security.[38] Among state departments, the police have led the way in setting up accounts with Sina Weibo and Tencent Weibo, with 4 000 police bureaus and 5 000 police officers registered.[39]

According to Chinese official media, the functions of government

Weibo accounts can be summarised as providing useful information and e-services; solving public relation crises; and handling negative news and refuting rumours.[40] The party-state considers tweets and status updates as a means of reducing strained relations between the state and the public, allowing officials to communicate at a grassroots level.[41] Officials use government Weibo accounts to hold online conferences and solicit public opinion about public matters like traffic rules, visa applications, household registration and fire prevention. By actively engaging with netizens on Weibo, the party-state can deliver its message directly, improve the state's image, as well as influence public opinion in a more effective way.

The CCP carries out a carrot-and-stick policy in managing netizens and Internet public opinion, encouraging free expression in non-sensitive areas but discouraging the expression of opinion in sensitive areas. While an increasing number of official scandals have been exposed through social media, the government has also launched a campaign against what it called online rumours. Hundreds of netizens across the country were arrested for spreading (allegedly false) rumours online. Meanwhile, the state media also warned opinion leaders on Weibo to watch their words.[42] Some of them were arrested. Among them were popular microbloggers with millions of followers on Weibo – the so-called 'Big Vs', whose identity or accounts have been verified. Charles Xue, a naturalised American with 12 million followers, was one of the Big Vs; he was accused of holding group sex parties with prostitutes.

The anti-rumour campaign was seen by some as an excuse to 'quash anti-government discourse'[43] and to 'tame the entire microblogging world'.[44] The government, however, emphasised its commitment to removing content it deemed critical or offensive from the web. The deputy director of the State Internet Information Office commented: 'the fight against rumours has received a positive response and has been quite effective ... the Internet has become clean.'[45]

As the authorities tightened up non-official channels, they also strengthened their efforts in combating corruption via official channels. In April 2013 news websites of major state media, such as Xinhua and the *People's Daily*, and mainstream commercial portal sites, such as Sina and Sohu, provided links to five government websites for reporting corruption. Traffic to the website set up by the CCP's Organisation Department increased from 6 000 per day to more than 20 000 and it received 100 tip-offs from netizens daily by September 2013.[46]

On 2 September 2013, five official websites dealing with anti-corruption were integrated into one and relaunched. The new website is smart phone- and tablet-friendly. An associated official Weibo account and Wechat service for mobile phone users were also scheduled to open later on.[47] The main website consists of ten sections, including information on anti-corruption campaigns and investigations, as well as an online forum for netizens for leaving comments, making proposals and filing inquiries.[48] One of the most important sections of the website is dedicated to reports of corruption cases where an informant may choose whether to report to the Central Commission for Discipline Inspection or its local branches, depending on the location of the informant.[49]

Instead of pushing reform, promoting greater transparency or enhancing government accountability, the emphasis of the CCP's Internet anti-corruption campaign is on encouraging netizens to report corruption via official channels rather than via social media. Corruption cases posted on social media can be read by everyone and disseminated in a split second, whereas cases reported on an official website cannot be seen by anyone other than the official handling the case. As well as an attempt to centralise the once decentralised anti-corruption platform, it is also a move to reduce the transparency of netizens' reports on corruption.

China's state media have called the new integrated anti-corruption website a 'regular army',[50] comparing it to the haphazard nature of non-official anti-corruption reports. This 'regular army' is said to minimise the chance of slander, sometimes characteristic of reports given through non-official channels.[51]

While social media platforms are run by commercial companies beyond the direct control of the state, the two strategies adopted by the CCP, of advocating e-government and encouraging netizens to participate in combating corruption, are the party's attempts to bring the public to its own websites. As the common wisdom goes, 'if you can't beat them, join them'. Embracing social media, such as by setting up accounts on Weibo to interact with netizens, shows the authorities' pragmatic approach to ICT. In this way, the CCP has managed to maintain its dominance over society.

Transformation of party–government relations

The Chinese state is a part of the CCP, as the party creates the state.[52] All proactive Internet measurements that are introduced are designed to guarantee the dominance of the party over the state. What the Internet has done is to empower the party to control the government and promote better governance. Studies found that the legitimacy of state institutions with which ordinary people interact, such as cadres, police and local government, was considerably lower than that of the central government, with which they have no contact.[53] Moreover, political support among rural dwellers declined from 50 per cent for the central party-state to 25, five, two and one per cent for the next four administrative levels: provincial, municipal, county and township.[54] In an effort to counteract these trends, government Weibo has become increasingly popular among the local party-state, with new accounts set up every day.[55]

Describing the Internet as a whole, Jiang suggests that the Chinese government consciously allows the public a limited amount of freedom on issues of economic, social, and political affairs in order to reduce social discontent and channel online public opinion in support of government policies and agendas.[56] Jiang's observation is particularly true of the government's approach towards Weibo. Besides serving people's practical needs, the government at the higher level uses Weibo as a platform to build up an image of accountability at the expense of government at the lower level. Government scandals exposed by Weibo users take place below provincial level, mostly at county level; issues addressed by government Weibo are not politically sensitive. The wrongdoing of village or county officials is allowed to be exposed on Weibo, and then the mayor, governor or party secretary acts as a tribune to help the aggrieved citizens. The following is an example.

In September 2010, three members of the Zhong family set themselves on fire in front of county officials in protest at the forced demolition of their home. When the self-immolation failed to convince the county government to back down, two of the Zhong sisters decided to fly to Beijing to petition the government but were stopped at the local airport by dozens of county officials. With the help of netizens and journalists via Weibo, their case reached the attention of officials at the municipal and then provincial level.[57] Seven officials from Yihuang county have been punished by the provincial party committee for mishandling the demolition, and both the party secretary and county governor were dismissed.

Research has shown that better access to government information and increased transparency through the use of ICT increase trust among citizens. A study of the potential impacts of ICT (in particular, e-government and social media) on cultural attitudes towards government suggests that social technologies can promote openness, transparency and reduce corruption.[58] E-government can be defined as 'utilizing the Internet and the World-Wide-Web for delivering government information and services to citizens'.[59] It is estimated that China has invested one trillion yuan in e-government initiatives at all administrative levels, and the annual budget for e-government is estimated to be growing at around 40 per cent a year.[60] This massive investment in e-government initiatives is unprecedented among developing nations. Far more resources in China are devoted to building the infrastructure, mandating officials to use the Internet and encouraging online participation than are spent on the mechanisms of control. Enhancing government performance, reducing tension between state and society, and fostering economic growth through the promotion of e-government can all be considered proactive strategies by an authoritarian regime.[61]

The Chinese government launched the Golden Projects in 1993

to build a sophisticated information network throughout China and set up 'Government Online Projects' to promote the application of Internet-based technology at all levels of government.[62] More and more state departments have established websites or uploaded databases and archives on the web. In 2007 China's State Council adopted regulations on Open Government Information that require government offices at each administrative level to disclose government information and annual reports. According to the regulations, the purpose of the open information initiative was to 'enhance the transparency of the work of government, promote administration in accordance with the law, and bring into full play the role of government information in serving the people's production and livelihood and their economic and social activities'.[63]

The CCP has utilised the opportunity brought by the rapid development of ICT and pushed forward e-government programmes nationwide. In addition to enhancing the quality of government service and improving decision-making processes by increasing government capacity, e-government can also promote anti-corruption drives and better accountability.[64] The CCP has extended e-government to the fight against crime, and against corruption in particular. This not only meets the demand of public opinion but also serves as a way for the central leadership to control the state. Corruption is one of the problems the CCP has faced ever since the establishment of the People's Republic in 1949. With the introduction of reforms and an open-door policy in 1978, China has experienced rapid economic growth. One of the inevitable by-products of a socialist market economy is widespread corruption. Although CCP's top leaders have over the past three decades emphasised the importance of combating corruption and launched a series of anti-corruption campaigns, the situation did not improve considerably. According to the Corruption Perceptions Index (CPI) published by Transparency International, China's ranking in the world has been on a steady decline, from 41st in 1997 to 80th in 2013,[65] indicating deteriorating international perceptions.

ICT plays an increasing role in fighting corruption worldwide.

In fact, the CCP has recognised the significance of the Internet in this respect for several years. The Supreme People's Procuratorate established a team in 2008 that specialises in collecting corruption data as well as monitoring online public opinion on corruption issues.[66] In 2010, the CCP's Central Commission for Discipline Inspection (CCDI) called for the expansion of (online) channels to make it easier for people to participate in fighting corruption.[67] China's first white paper on corruption, which was released at the end of 2010, reiterated the importance of the Internet as a new tool in the campaign against corruption.[68]

It has become a norm in the post-Deng Xiaoping era that whoever succeeds as China's top leader takes a strong position in fighting corruption at the beginning of their term. Punishing corrupt officials and pushing an anti-corruption campaign also help establish the authority of the central government as well as the new leader. Jailing 'corrupt' officials is at the same time a common expression of party infighting and the reshuffling of power within its ranks. In this view, fighting corruption can be seen as a double-edged sword: not only is the new leader seen as tough on corruption, but he also consolidates power by removing political opponents. However, such campaigns fail to protect ordinary citizens from corruption, especially at the local governance level.

Although Jiang, Hu and Xi have each brought down a member of the CCP's Politburo on corruption charges, without genuine political reform and independent media to provide checks and balances the effectiveness of the campaign is questionable. While the party-state found it difficult, if not impossible, to control social media, it utilised the opportunities brought by ICT to centralise an anti-corruption platform to serve its interests. By promoting Internet anti-corruption efforts and encouraging the general public to participate in it, the CCP under Xi's leadership has projected an image of caring for people's concerns and combating corruption.

Conclusion

The Internet has diversified information sources and changed the information flow from one-way to two-way. Public opinion formulated in the cyberworld has translated into public pressure and, on many occasions, brought down corrupt officials or forced the party-state to adjust its policies. Although ICT have given netizens more leverage to influence state's policies, it has also provided the party-state with new opportunities to utilise the Internet to better serve the people and direct public opinion, increase transparency and promote better governance.

The Chinese government started to build a sophisticated information network as early as 1993 and began conducting Government Online Projects to promote the application of Internet-based technology at all levels of government. By the end of 2013, nearly all government departments at every administrative level have set up official websites. Better access to government information and increased transparency through the use of ICTs has increased trust among citizens.

The CCP has recognised the importance of the Internet as a new tool in fighting corruption. It has tried to centralise the way anti-corruption investigations are conducted by discouraging the public exposure of officials' wrongdoing via social media and urging netizens to report corruption cases to the state directly through the government website. By promoting Internet anti-corruption efforts and encouraging the general public to participate, the CCP projected an image of sharing a common goal with the people. In short, the party-state's capacity to dominate society and strengthen itself in delivering public services has been enhanced with the help of the Internet.

The Internet, to a large extent, has empowered both the party-state and society. The promotion of e-government and the popularisation of Weibo have contributed to political openness, transparency and accountability. These are important aspects of political liberalisation: the party-state has become more accountable to the people and is willing to compromise with public opinion. Nonetheless, political liberalisation has not yet led to political democratisation: the latter involves a fundamental reform of the current political structure which might threaten the rule of the CCP, something the party will not tolerate.

At the party–government level, the Internet has enabled the CCP leadership to exert better control on local government as well as consolidate the CCP's central authority. The role of ICT in mobilising public support, guiding public opinion in the government's favour and improving the CCP's legitimacy is becoming more and more important. As Weibo has increasingly emerged as a significant news source about social discontent, the CCP has allowed free debate on issues concerning local government while closely monitoring and restricting any discussion on sensitive topics related to top-level leadership and governance. The central government has allowed netizens to exercise pressure on local government on certain local issues in order to consolidate the rule of central government.

The CCP has shown its ability to adapt and accommodate the new Internet environment in order to guarantee its domination over state and society. 'The interactive process between the state and society is mutually transformative', as Zheng puts it.[69] The CCP has transformed itself in line with ICT development while maintaining its domination over the state, society and the Internet. All the same, the whole picture of the political impact of ICT on the CCP has yet to be fully revealed.

7
Factional dynamics in the Indian National Congress and the African National Congress

Thiven Reddy

In the 2014 general elections India witnessed the decimation of the Indian National Congress (INC) at the polls. The end of the INC as a dominant party could not have been more final, though we can trace its decline as far back as the 1967 elections. The electoral rout of the INC can be explained by the economic woes of high inflation and price rises, leadership weaknesses, corruption and unclear party–state relations.[1] Yet besides these more immediate factors the decline of the INC is not unrelated to organisational weaknesses in the party developing over many decades, which provide the theme of this chapter.

That the once-admired institutional strengths of the INC as the leader of the nationalist struggle were allowed to erode suggests fruitful comparisons with the changing fortunes of the African National Congress (ANC) in South Africa. Though the ANC has just won another comfortable general election, in May 2014, it too displays trends of institutional weakness, exemplified in heightened factional conflict and growing mass discontent in a democracy that remains constantly in trouble, not unlike the India of the 1980s.

This chapter compares the INC and ANC as party organisations. In particular it focuses on internal factional dynamics, a key indicator of party organisational strength accounting for party dominance in their political contexts. Drawing on Boucek's[2] basic classification of factionalism into three types – cooperative, competitive and degenerative – I argue that national liberation movements that obtain their legitimacy from mass social mobilisation are inherently prone to factionalism. Once in control of the state, the emergence of 'two centres of power'[3] within the party, the party bureaucracy and the party-in-government, produces conditions for competitive and ultimately degenerative factional dynamics which previous mechanisms of factional management are unable to contain effectively. In the years of nationalist struggle, we witness a form of factional dynamics that approximates the cooperative and competitive types of factionalism; once nationalist movements occupy state power for extended periods of time, the 'degenerative factionalism' type comes to the fore because of the tensions between the two wings of the dominant party.

Factional dynamics and dominant party systems

Boucek's typology of factional dynamics offers a helpful point of departure and moves us beyond the simplistic assumption that some political parties are factionalised and others are not or, at least, are insignificantly factionalised. In her scheme, cooperative factionalism refers to the formative period when a democracy or a party is establishing itself.[4] The formative context requires that diverse intra-party groups work with each other in pursuit of the larger goal. The incentive to cooperate motivates different interests to find a common voice; in this sense factionalism is positive, allowing for the opinions and interests of various sectional interests to be 'mobilized within a single organisation'.[5] As a feature and process, factionalism allows interest groups to remain separate, to retain their identities and at the same time to influence outcomes towards the larger goal. This process of 'give and take' makes for a consensus-building mode of politics and also helps educate memberships in compromise and negotiated outcomes.

The second type, competitive factionalism, involving 'fragmentation and splits',[6] differs from the first in that factions approach each other not merely to retain separate identities, but to oppose each other and achieve factional goals. To decide when one or the other type obtains is potentially the source of much debate; retaining separate identities and engaging in conflict are claims subject to empirical context, question of degree, and interpretation. For instance, the ideological differences within the ANC over macroeconomic policy during the Mbeki period have been likened to the conflict between two 'opposition parties' within the same organisation. It is difficult to determine whether this amounts to a situation of factional competition or factional degeneration. The consequences can be both positive and negative. On the positive side factionalism encourages more internal debate, enhancing party democracy,[7] yet detrimentally it can produce paralysis, making decisive policy formulation impossible, fragmenting party allegiances, and producing the conditions for a split in the organisation. The crucial variables preventing competitive factionalism from becoming degenerative and eventually destructive are the timely, pragmatic and considered interventionist role of factional elites, appropriate party structures and rules and their application within the party to discourage such outcomes.

The third type, degenerative factionalism, occurs when factionalism becomes destructive, threatening the coherence and stability of the party. In this type, factions embed themselves deeply in the party organisation, use their factional strength to win positions and posts in the state, accumulate spoils, and exchange these resources for grassroots support. This type of politics fuels extensive corruption, as 'vertical networks of political patronage' from state to society produce a form of politics in which public resources are exchanged for support. As state resources are limited, factional conflict increases in intensity, eventually becoming unsustainable without destroying the party organisation. In South Africa this type of politics has been manifested in the ever-widening number of cabinet posts. The ANC has steadily increased the number of cabinet posts from the Mandela to the Zuma governments because the party leader remains obligated to widen his support by satisfying the various factions within the party through patronage.[8]

Perhaps because Boucek's cases are limited to Italy and Japan, features of degenerative factionalism as she describes them are restricted entirely to elite behaviour outside the context of mass participatory democracy. In this chapter we are dealing with the case of dominant parties emerging out of nationalist, anti-colonial struggles involving mass social mobilisation. Once such movements have achieved power, the glue that held the constituent disparate elements together dissolves and the access to state power opens up deep tensions between elites in control of the machinery of the state and those in control of the party machine. Whereas during the period of social mobilisation decision-making was firmly confined to the upper tiers of the party organisation, now those who have achieved power in the state feel hampered by party interference, arguing that the business of daily administration requires immediate responses and different kinds of knowledge. Those in control of the party, on the other hand, feel undermined, and believe that party democracy is being bypassed by 'unaccountable' state leaders.

The role of the charismatic leader somewhat moderates these party–state tensions. Both Nehru and Mandela had to overcome these tensions, and their pragmatic style and individual charisma contributed to their effectiveness in doing so. In the Indian case, the tensions between Nehru and Patel were expressed in the post-independence period in presidential leadership contests, as we shall see below.[9] In South Africa this tension between the 'two centres of power' came to the fore in the Mbeki and Zuma factional battles. But in South Africa, unlike India, because the former colonisers remained in the country and continued to hold the dominant position in all spheres except formal political power, the two wings of the ruling party require each other. Ideological differences over specific policy issues play a role in factional competition, but the real battles are over spoils.[10] Since politics is a crucial means for upward social mobility, these battles over spoils that control of the state allows increase factional competition. The immense predictability of election outcomes for the dominant party shifts the competition for state positions into the party.

In India, during the period of unstable INC rule from 1969 onwards, and in South Africa, especially during Mbeki's second term as president, degenerative factionalism can be associated with the 'criminalisation of politics' and a form of relationship between state and society that approaches the condition of 'politics without administration'. Factional battles in the dominant party become endemic. Because the goal of holding onto political power is so attractive and the material rewards so great, coalition politics are extremely unstable and governments at regional and especially local levels are continually falling apart. Under these conditions party and ethnic elites make appeals to the masses to support their particular interests: this serves to undermine formal institutions, and administrative action becomes more and more ineffective. Writing about the India of the 1980s, Singh notes that the 'administration without politics' syndrome may begin with some effective measures to curb corruption, administrative inefficiency, and economic decline, but in the absence of democratic feedback it degenerates into unmitigated repression, corruption in high places and ego-inflation on a mammoth scale.[11] In this situation of political decay, formal and informal processes of politics become less distinguishable, and 'money and muscle power' take hold of politics.

The nationalist struggle and cooperative factional dynamics

In the deeply divided societies of colonial India and South Africa, nationalist parties were inevitably faction-ridden.[12] Making the claim of representing the nation credible required that nationalist organisations assume an ideologically flexible approach, embracing a wide range of constituencies. They needed to adapt to diverse regional and local cultural interests as well as negotiate the multiple identities of class, caste, race and language groups. In India and South Africa the nationalist movement grew steadily from its beginnings as a small middle-class group, which, after eventually realising that colonial power was not going to be bent by their limited efforts, saw in mass mobilisation the answer to a successful strategy of resistance.[13] The harsher and longer the colonial form of domination, the more complex the relationship between the masses and the dominant parties became, involving a complex discourse about colonial oppression, resistance and post-colonial development. The INC and ANC are institutional expressions of this broader discourse of nationalist resistance, a discourse about resisting colonialism and going beyond it, discourses that are central to understanding post-colonial party systems. To those factors that account for party dominance, we need to add this 'cultural meaning', the material-symbolic value of citizen identity formation associated with nationalist struggles against colonialism, which are characterised by the pragmatic acceptance of broad coalitions to represent the nation. The politics of mass social mobilisation characteristic of nationalist struggles promoted an internal dynamic that allowed for the acceptance of factional differences and also a willingness to manage factional cooperation and moderate competition.

Three interrelated elements of the INC and the ANC – the legitimacy that comes from a legacy of anti-colonial struggle, impressive adaptive capacities in response to a changing political terrain, and the ability to keep the organisation internally coherent by effectively managing internal party conflict – help us grasp how and why these nationalist movements became the central expression of post-colonial social transformation in their societies. No doubt a large role was played by elites. In the anti-colonial struggle they valued charismatic politics, pragmatic ideology, and a willingness to adapt the organisation. Joshi and Desai emphasise this flexibility and openness of the INC: 'its open-umbrella character, its power and patronage after independence, its expanding social base due to social co-optation and factional competition – all these factors were responsible for the growth of the Congress into a dominant party, reflecting a national consensus'.[14]

Nationalist resistance required that the elites develop not only strong links with the masses, but, more importantly, incentives not to allow their own factional differences to disturb the prevailing spirit of cooperation. As Joshi and Hebsur remark of the INC, 'The party developed a unique knack of harbouring almost irreconcilable elements,'[15] such as the strong differences between liberal moderates and socialists. It is important to remember that during the nationalist struggle many strategic issues could easily have become the basis for factional splits; for example, what tactics to adopt for effective popular mobilisation, or whether to participate in colonial political structures after the 1936 Constitution.

Until Gandhi's participation, the INC was unable to transcend its narrow social base. Gandhi's charismatic intervention transformed Congress into a mass organisation. He moulded complex modernist and Hindu ideas, practices and symbols into a mobilising force. Congress was reorganised and slowly began to move beyond its traditional upper-caste membership to include the rural masses, untouchables, lower castes and women. Gandhi's 'politics of consensus' downplayed the class contradictions in Congress, cultivating a diverse support base with such effect that the organisation is often described as radical in rhetoric but moderate in practice, a result of this mediation between different constituencies.

The politics of mass mobilisation waged against colonialism left the Congress a strong organisation with practices and structures directed towards party management. As an organisation it had to become more formidable than the structures of the colonial state; in time it mirrored the state and established branches throughout the country, aiming to mobilise supporters from the village level upwards. The key structure, 'the highest executive authority of Congress', was the Working Committee.[16] This committee, also known as the High Command or Syndicate, 'aided materially in the transformation of Congress from an independence movement to a governing political party and contributed to its dominance during the first two decades following the transfer of power'. As members of the committee a core group of veteran Congress leaders who tended to be longstanding members of parliament, government ministers and chief ministers served regularly. This was the body responsible for managing internal party conflict, providing the government with broad policy guidelines, managing the relationship between the party and the government, and selecting candidates (nominated from lower structures) for all national and state structures.[17] During the period of national liberation the Working

Committee was vital in inculcating factional cooperation, by focusing on the enemy of colonialism and mobilising diverse groups against it.

The Congress system and competitive factional dynamics

The INC had been in existence for 62 years at the time of independence and the ANC for 82 years when it came to power. Time provides skills in how to survive and adapt to changing contexts, allows for the development of a strong enough institutional base to constitute the identity of its members, and brings with it the necessary legitimacy conducive for the stability and consolidation of the new democratic institutions. But in contributing towards the new political system and managing the transition to independence, the INC was far more successful than in anticipating how control of the state would impact on factional dynamics within the party.

The success of the INC in transforming itself from a nationalist resistance movement to a governing political party was indicative of its degree of institutionalisation (developed during the struggle period) and, consequently, its capacity to adapt to a changing political environment. According to Kothari,[18] the INC's participation in colonial structures provided an important learning experience in governance. The party readily accepted the electoral system and prepared for regular elections, gradually transforming its structures into powerful instruments of electoral campaigning. It did not abandon its attention to organisation, though now its structures of popular mobilisation for protest were turned into structures of popular mobilisation for votes. Ideologically, the party upheld its belief in democratic norms and respect for the rule of law, and made every effort to emphasise its role as a torchbearer of democracy. The sensitivity of the partition process made it acutely aware of the need to prevent civil strife, even if state repression was required to put down communal conflict.

Nehru, like Mandela in South Africa, has been given credit for his role in the transition in India. Nehru confronted the issue of effective relations between the party and government, made the transition from nationalist movement to ruling party easier, and managed relations between Congress and opposition parties. Within the INC, Nehru followed a nuanced path between factions pulling in different directions, though he was unable to control the Congress party machine until after the death of his main rival, Sardar Patel. For Weiner,[19] besides Nehru's personal charisma and his role in Congress during the struggle for independence, the success of post-independence India was due to the political elites as a whole. What was crucial was the ability and desire of Congress leaders to do 'whatever [was] necessary to adapt the party to its environment'.[20]

The first five years after independence were marked by the management of factionalism through the Congress system and elite consensus.[21] The term 'Congress system' has been developed to understand INC dominance once in power, by relating internal factionalism to politics outside the organisation, thereby accounting for the articulation and aggregation of societal interests under single-party dominance.[22] While the Indian party system did not ignore the value of party competition, the regular electoral victories of Congress pointed to the absence of the usual alternation of governing parties characteristic of other democratic states. Morris-Jones succinctly describes this system as 'dominance coexisting with competition but without a trace of alternation'.[23]

The INC's dominant position can be explained by the structure and composition of the dominant party in receptively allowing for the factional representation of competing societal interests. At the same time, the different opposition parties, civil society associations and influential charismatic leaders in society were encouraged to articulate their views and interests through the dominant party. In addition, the various factions of the dominant party themselves helped to organise and represent different interests, thereby extending the reach of the INC deep into civil society. Lal[24] writes about factions extending all the way into remote villages, helping to cut across cleavages of class, religion and caste, and, most importantly, allowing space for new leadership to emerge. INC factional identities tended to be fluid, and as these extended into society they helped bring large swathes of historically marginalised people into the political system. According to Kaviraj,[25] the predisposition of the ruling party to assume 'the centre' of the ideological and policy spectrum, despite itself containing diverse viewpoints, forced opposition parties into the margins. 'The one-party dominant system had, from the start, made ideological opposition unnecessary to some extent, as interests of both leftist and rightist politics could be articulated through groups inside the Congress itself.' This description, it should be noted, no longer applies to Indian politics, which are far more adversarial. The end of INC dominance and of the Congress system brought with it a proliferation of regional parties, enabling them to bargain with national parties through pragmatic coalitions.

But while, in the initial post-independence period, factions retained their identities and competed with each other within the framework of the INC, the internal dynamics of the party took strain around the question of the 'two centres of power'. When the Nehru government increasingly began to bypass the party organisation in policy decision-making, Patel, who controlled the party machinery, led the charge to restore the party's former influence. This tension between party and state leadership and between Patel and Nehru expressed itself in the selection of the party president in 1950. Of the two candidates Patel supported the conservative Tandon, while Nehru backed the long-time Gandhist and socialist Kripalani. After a bruising process Tandon won.[26] This factional conflict did not end with the presidential elections, continuing with the selection of candidates for the Central Election Committee, the structure responsible for selecting candidates for national and state elections.

Shortly after Patel's death in 1950, Nehru attempted to resolve the party–state conflict by introducing procedures for party presidential selection that would avoid a repetition of the Tandon–Kripalani conflict. He became key in selecting the Congress president, relying on consensus in the party while also giving consideration to regional balance, minority representation, development of new leaders and previous government experience.[27] In this sense factionalism was accepted, competition allowed, but it was all managed by the National Working Committee and by national and regional elites.

Dominant party decline of the INC

The ending of INC dominance can be attributed to changes in the broader polity, particularly the politicisation at the state level of previously marginalised groups, as well as internal organisational factors. The post-independence political elite identified the goals of modern India as universal suffrage, development planning, secularisation, and the elimination of caste practices in favour of modern citizenship. This script of modernisation dominated thinking about development in the first two decades after independence. Under circumstances where the masses left politics to the elites, this dominant approach remained stable, but the broader social changes in the late 1960s ended this elite consensus.[28]

At the same time, the death of the old guard inspired different ideologies and a new type of politics. With a split in the Communist Party and the decline of right-wing politics, Congress was left without left and right factions. Then in the mid-1970s under Indira Gandhi the country was subjected to an Indian variant of authoritarianism. All of these factors hastened the fragmentation of the party system of contemporary Indian politics.

Kaviraj emphasises the 'unexpected and unprecedented change'[29] that Indian society experienced in the late 1960s, a 'structural crisis … one major feature of [which] was the increasing strain on the secular form of the state and its formal constitution'.[30] It was a crisis that the Congress party was unable to control. The crucial issue for the Congress majority was discrimination against minorities; this eventually produced strong state parties with significant bargaining power. In terms of the constitution, minorities had certain rights, yet they still experienced enormous discrimination, while the Hindu majority complained that minorities were benefiting from advantages derived from their constitutional status. The other crisis that the party faced was more internal in origin. The increasing control of the Nehru–Gandhi family of the INC and their domination of its leadership structures pointed to institutional weaknesses of party organisation. In formal terms, the Congress Party might appear to be a mass party, but in reality it was a cadre party with a prominent popular leader.

In what can be seen as a case study of degenerative factionalism, Congress suffered a break-up in 1969, in a situation that replayed the earlier tension between state and party evident in the Nehru–Patel disputes of the 1950s. As with the ANC before the removal of Thabo Mbeki at the ANC's Polokwane conference,[31] in the months preceding the split in the INC, tensions between the 'two centres of power' mounted. The office of the prime minister was involved in regular disputes with the leaders in the party organisation, who felt increasingly marginalised by the government leadership. These party leaders, who had established national and regional bases of support, known as the Syndicate, questioned and challenged the authority of the prime ministership, wanting to reverse Indira Gandhi's dominance over the party.

In response to the increasing political consciousness of the electorate and the growing inequality between the poor and the traditional Congress support base of wealthy peasants and landowners, Indira Gandhi had embarked on a campaign committed to socialism, calling for nationalisation of the major commercial banks, radical land reforms, limits on urban incomes and some restrictions on the major industrial concerns.[32] She also wanted to re-establish the power of the prime ministership vis-à-vis the Syndicate. These ideological and political differences between the leaders in government and those in the organisation came to a head over the selection of the candidate list for the 1972 elections and especially the position of the president of the country.

At a meeting in July 1969, the two sides differed strongly on the choice of presidential candidate. Indira Gandhi initially proposed the candidacy of V.V. Giri, who stood as an independent and received support from socialists and communists. The Syndicate, on the other hand, wanted the conservative Sanjiva Reddy to be elected.[33] Despite the party leadership instructing all Congress members of parliament to elect Reddy, Indira Gandhi refused to follow the whip's orders, and called for a free vote among her supporters. Giri won the election. Although the Working Committee made a plea for party unity, the Syndicate demanded disciplinary action against the prime minister. Indira Gandhi did not help matters or enhance party unity by immediately firing four junior ministers, all associated with the Syndicate. The Syndicate then responded by removing two members of the Working Committee sympathetic to Indira Gandhi's position, giving Syndicate supporters a majority on the committee. In a reversal of the Nehru-era situation in which the government dominated the party, the party now dominated the government.

The crisis came to a head when two separate meetings of the Working Committee took place – one under the auspices of the Syndicate and another at the home of Indira Gandhi. In November the regular Working Committee expelled Indira Gandhi, expecting the Congress Parliamentary Committee to elect a new leader, which this body refused to do, re-endorsing her leadership. The result was a split in the Indian Congress party, which ushered in the 'mass populism, authoritarianism and imperial premiership' of Indira Gandhi's government.[34] Although in the national elections of 1984, immediately following her assassination, the party received its highest percentage of the national vote, it had by then become highly corrupt, organisationally weak, racked by factional disputes, and in general a shadow of its former self. In the 1998 general election it recorded its lowest support ever, a drop of some 22 per cent in the intervening 12 years. Despite its reliance on coalitions, the INC was unable to establish its former glory and throughout the early 2000s held precariously onto power in two United Progressive Alliance governments. Its former dominance had become a thing of the past.

ANC and cooperative factional dynamics

The struggle for liberation in South Africa was fought by many organisations representing different ideologies, strategies and tactics and with different strengths and weaknesses.[35] But the combination within the ANC of its broad, inclusive character, its cultural symbolism, and long institutional history created a pool of adaptive capacities that enabled it to contain internal factional conflict and to out-compete its rivals in the nationalist struggle. Compared with its rivals, the ANC pursued pragmatic politics, followed a more inclusive ideology and was more open to negotiations with the apartheid regime. It proved institutionally stronger than rival organisations, which were unable to adapt or remain internally coherent, and, despite representing a wider ideological spectrum, managed its internal tensions pragmatically. The ANC emerged from the urban uprisings of the 1980s in better shape and entered into the politics of negotiations with renewed confidence.[36] On the other hand, its rivals were unable to agree on how to respond to F.W. de Klerk's reform initiatives, the content of democratic discourse, or details of the new constitution or deal tactically with important moments during the negotiations process.

It was widely expected that the ANC, as the leading organisation in the nationalist struggle, would assume control of the state after the first democratic election in 1994. After all, it had enjoyed an impressive level of legitimacy during the fight against apartheid colonialism and was the oldest political organisation in the country, going back to the very formation of the modern South African state in 1910. In the formative years of the democratic political system, the ANC's presence provided much-needed stability. The party bestowed legitimacy on the new political dispensation even though, or precisely because, the political system was the product of a negotiated settlement in which the ANC had agreed to significant compromises with white minority interests.

Nationalism, for the early ANC, was an elitist project.[37] The ANC's formation in 1912 saw a coming together of existing African organisations and civic bodies of chiefs, lawyers, journalists and clergymen. At first this emergent nationalist elite held a fairly limited understanding of the political participation of South Africa's African population. The objective of African nationalism was merely to extend the restrictive franchise that Africans enjoyed in the Cape Province – limited to African males who qualified on property and educational grounds – to similarly positioned individuals in the other provinces. During the course of the 20th century, the growth in industrialisation and the emergence of ideas about rights and democracy beyond a narrow elite of African society pressured the ANC to broaden its ideological stance. Before the Second World War ended, it adopted a document entitled 'African Claims' in which it demanded universal franchise and started to focus on popular pressure as a means to resist the white government's attempts to extend racial segregation.

In 1955 the ANC adopted the Freedom Charter, outlining broad democratic demands such as established liberal individual rights, but also envisioning wealth redistribution through nationalisation of key sectors of the economy. The Charter's breadth, it was hoped, would unite a diverse range of social forces in support of the ANC. In the late 1960s the ANC, now an outlawed organisation in South Africa, began to move ideologically leftwards under the influence of Third World liberation discourses after Bandung and more radical experiences in parts of Asia and Latin America. As the adoption of its Strategy and Tactics document at the Morogoro conference in 1969 indicated, it increasingly embraced class analysis of apartheid and developed a strategy of liberation emphasising 'people's war'. At the same time, at no stage did it abandon its self-conception as a multi-class nationalist movement encompassing various ideologies, traditions and ethnic or racial cultures. The ideological differences between the Africanists and Marxists continued to simmer in the organisation, though the pragmatic, Nehru-like interventions of its president, O.R. Tambo, for the most part kept these within limits.

One historical legacy of the ANC that stands out is that during the liberation period it retained a relative openness to differences, allowing for radically opposing ideological strands to be articulated within it. This accommodative approach to factional management was even more pronounced in the wide range of civil society organisations, supportive of the ANC, that came together as the United Democratic Front in the mid-1980s. Here, 'difference' was valued, and the experience gave material and institutional embodiment to a particular strand of struggle culture.

The history of domination that constituted people's subjectivities during the colonial era and under the apartheid regime continues to influence people's perceptions today. The discourse of the struggle for liberation frames, to a degree, the political culture of contemporary South African politics in that opposition to the ANC can easily be painted as preserving narrow white-minority interests. This tension between remembering the past and facing the contradictions of the present is such that citizens can both identify with and remain loyal to the dominant party and at the same time be strongly critical towards it. The centrifugal social forces that produced multiple regional and local political parties in India have not yet taken root in South Africa.

ANC in government: Competitive and degenerative factional dynamics

During the immediate post-1994 period, the ANC took for granted its capacity to manage internal rivalries effectively, despite important regional and ideological differences. Even though factional tensions were evident during Mandela's term in office, disputes became more open under the leadership of President Mbeki. In this period we can identify factionalism as intensely competitive and perhaps as degenerative.[38] The consensus that characterised the party during the early years of democracy began to wane. Thus, while the ANC's degree of institutionalisation has greatly contributed to its dominant position, there are clearly visible signs that it faces tremendous strains.

Factional conflict has become in fact endemic in the ANC. Indeed, factional interests have always been represented by the ANC's relations with its allies, the Congress of South African Trade Unions (Cosatu) and the South African Communist Party (SACP), and further complicated by factional identities within these and other ANC structures. During the Mandela era, Bantu Holomisa was expelled from the party after he refused to apologise for accusing a fellow cabinet minister of corruption,[39] and went on to form his own party, the United Democratic Movement. As it does not significantly differ on ideological grounds with the mainstream in the ANC, it could be viewed as a faction drawn largely from the region of the Transkei.

In the early to mid-1990s some considered the ANC's dominance to be unproblematic, assuming that the different factions would cooperate and this would enhance internal debate and openness and overall stability. This changed under the leadership of President Thabo Mbeki, who centralised power and discouraged dissent, drawing precisely on the values of party discipline to enforce internal unity. But the Mbeki years were in fact a time of intense factional conflict, which the key structures of the organisation, the NWC and NEC, found it difficult to control, as these bodies themselves came under the control of one or other faction.

The main conflict centred on Mbeki and his deputy president, Jacob Zuma, and was driven by the role of Zuma and his financial adviser Schabir Shaik in the corruption scandal surrounding the arms deal. At its core the real dispute centred on relations between the state leadership and those in the party machinery who felt the government was bypassing party structures in its decision-making. When Shaik was found guilty of a corrupt relationship with Zuma, Mbeki fired Zuma as the country's deputy president. The party leadership and machinery then supported Zuma, believing that Mbeki was using the state to fight factional battles in the ANC.[40] The factional conflict between Mbeki and Zuma from 2001 onwards took many legal twists and political turns, ultimately affecting judicial, state and civil society institutions negatively. The dramatic showdown at the ANC's national conference in Polokwane, the victory of the Zuma faction in party elections, the recall of Mbeki as president and the formation of a splinter party of Mbeki loyalists, the Congress of the People (Cope), all demonstrate the degenerative features of factionalism.

Ideological differences over approaches to post-apartheid development have also fuelled factional divisions in the ANC. In 1994 the ANC embarked on the Reconstruction and Development Programme (RDP) as its main policy framework to overcome widespread poverty and inequality.[41] The RDP, so the ANC claimed, would redistribute wealth to poor people through extensive state intervention. But within two years, under pressure from the World Bank and the IMF, the ANC leadership abandoned the RDP and embraced the Growth, Employment and Redistribution (Gear) strategy, which amounted to a domestically designed structural adjustment programme.[42] The ruling party's economic policy has been lauded by the South African business sector, and strong ties between the ANC and business developed under Thabo Mbeki's leadership. At the same time, poor service delivery led to a series of protests, creating new tensions in the ANC, and between the ANC and its alliance partners Cosatu and the SACP. Although the ANC provides a massive social welfare programme for the least well-off and the government claims to promote a 'developmental state,' the ANC's alliance partners, particularly some elements in Cosatu, have remained uncomfortable with the lack of radical redistribution of wealth.

The inability of ANC decision-making structures – the NWC, NEC and the national conference – to effectively manage factional politics has weakened the organisation and its ability to govern. Whether because of a lack of state capacity, inefficiencies and corrupt practices, macroeconomic policies or party factionalism, citizens' frustrations with poor service delivery have steadily grown. This has resulted in increased social mobilisation, which in turn has put pressure on the ANC. The party's response is ambiguous. On the one hand, the ANC, as the leading organisation in a broad democratic movement promising a 'national democratic revolution', encourages political and social mobilisation, but, on the other hand, as the ruling party, the ANC falls back on a defensive approach that emphasises the 'rule of law'. The ANC's main defensive response seems to be to draw attention to ongoing racial divisions that have their roots in the apartheid past, thus evoking the struggle history that is the basis for its legitimacy and popularity. This strategy assists the ruling party by legitimising its dominant position but it also gives rise to a racialised political discourse that runs the risk of further radicalising and alienating the already discontented. The stark visibility of social relations that still mirror apartheid's socio-economic inequalities and the (partial) failure of the ANC to systematically address them have created a fertile ground for a sustainable racial discourse, which, in turn, ambiguously contributes to the ANC's dominant position.

Conclusion

The successes of national liberation movements that come to power primarily with the support of mass social mobilisation cannot be denied. Yet these movements, once in control of the state, are immediately confronted with the tensions between party members in government and those in control of the party organisation. The approach to factionalism that largely accounted for the success of their social mobilisation during the resistance phase comes under pressure in the post-liberation period and results in the beginnings of degenerative factionalism and a politics that undermines a democratic polity.

From the comparison of the ANC and INC, we can draw out three themes in relation to the dominant party literature. The first addresses the question of legitimacy, a widespread acceptance of the dominant party that comes from its role in anti-colonial struggle. Second, these old organisations claim to embody 'the nation' and do so by mobilising diverse sectors representative of broader society, which express themselves in factions. Throughout its resistance period it works out internal mechanisms to manage factional disputes, balancing party discipline with internal openness. Factional dynamics are cooperative. Once in power, however, the tensions between party and state and weak factional management result in dominant-party decline. In this period factional dynamics become competitive and eventually degenerative.

The source of the intensification of factional conflict lies in state resources and the promotion of patronage as a central means to conduct politics: this gradually displaces the party as the central locus of power. In the Indian case the social changes and Indira Gandhi's authoritarianism failed to respond adequately to party–state tensions, resulting in the splitting of the organisation. In South Africa the social pressures from frustrated citizen expectations, as well as Mbeki's approach to 'modernise' the organisation, alienated significant factional groups by breaking with the older, established pragmatic approach. In India the fragmentation of parties into smaller parties, the emergence of regional political parties, and local parties have become features of its political system. The question is whether this faction-produced fragmentation can also occur in South Africa. Whereas the trend towards fragmentation in India was partly due to a general consensus over the national questions, in contemporary South Africa national disputes over identity remain prominent, and because the struggle against white hegemony continues to have adherence, this may allow the ANC a degree of consensus on which to build.

In the case of the INC, factional management in the period of nationalist resistance was impressive, yet once it came to power competitive and degenerative factionalism became the norm. In the case of the ANC, it would seem, the party is in the degenerative phase of factional dynamics, which accounts for its institutional decline and declining moral legitimacy despite the handsome support it receives from the mass of South Africans at the polls.

8

Party–state relations in South Africa in a period of transition

Vinothan Naidoo

This chapter looks at the relationship between party and state in the context of state transformation in South Africa.* The incumbency of the African National Congress (ANC) since South Africa's democratisation in 1994 provides ample opportunity to examine how internally generated aims that accompanied the party's transition to power have affected externally directed efforts to transform the state machinery. As political parties have historically become increasingly organised and bureaucratised, they have emerged as influential actors in mediating the relationship between public accountability and the web of state institutions they oversee, for explicitly partisan ends. This scenario has been especially acute in the South African political system, in which state administration has, both prior to and after 1994, functioned in a highly partisan environment, and in which a dominant political party has exerted considerable control over the state.

Despite significant shifts in the policy agenda after the democratic transition, successive ANC governments have, like their National Party predecessors, faced regular public scrutiny and criticism for presiding over a state machinery that is poorly insulated and capacitated, as

---

* I would like to acknowledge the assistance of Mr Senzo Hlophe, a master's student in the Department of Political Studies, UCT, for his efforts in collecting and collating internal ANC documentation cited in this chapter.

measured by such indicators as service delivery performance[1] and corruption. This has often been linked to the party's explicit policy of 'deploying' its partisans in the offices of state institutions. On the one hand, the concept and practice of deployment is condemned as detrimental to cultivating a professional state administration, as well as contrary to the law. On the other hand, the deployment of 'cadres' is seen not merely as an administrative exercise, coinciding with a policy of state 'transformation' that includes making the bureaucracy more racially representative, but also represents a practical application of the ANC's liberation narrative in which the revolutionary demands of an opposition organisation were transmitted into policy initiatives once it assumed the reins of government. The most interesting space for analytical enquiry is probably the area between these two views, where debate has been sparked about whether the practice of deployment in the state via the party should be regulated, and how; and whether it is possible to seek a balance between political reliability and administrative proficiency.

The available evidence suggests that although the ANC has for a long time openly and explicitly advocated a policy of deployment in state institutions, this has in practice been implemented in a more discreet and less overt manner, although there are notable exceptions at the local government level. While this may be partially explained as an attempt by the party to signal a commitment to building a professional state bureaucracy, it might also be indicative of the party's inability to centrally orchestrate and control deployment across a multiplicity of institutions, including local government. The obscurity of its implementation also makes it difficult to gauge the extent of the party's direct reach into the state and the effects of this; despite some attempts to do so,[2] there is a dearth of empirical evidence to match more extensive normative critiques.

Deployment in historical context

This section will discuss the emergence and application of deployment as a core instrument of the ANC's transition from a liberation movement to governing party in the early to mid-1990s. It will also examine the relationship between the policy imperative of 'transforming' state institutions and the initial and explicit articulation by the ANC of a policy of developing and 'deploying' cadres, or party loyalists, into state institutions.

The ANC's strategy of deployment is well documented.[3] It has its roots in the party's cadre strategy, which predates the ANC's assumption of political power in 1994 and goes back to the organisation's 1985 national consultative conference in Kabwe, Zambia.[4] The conference proceedings speak explicitly of a 'cadre policy' as an instrument of strengthening the organisation, although the context is one of a government-in-waiting: articulating clear guidelines on the characteristics of a party cadre is considered crucial for the party's ability to demonstrate and prepare for political leadership. The profile of a cadre at this stage is noteworthy for its wide scope, which encompassed both military and civilian operatives, and emphasised the recruitment of women, young people (students) and those with specialised skills. 'Deployment' was just one of four so-called 'principles of work' that should apply to a cadre, the others being processes governing recruitment, education and training, and promotion and accountability. The key requirement of a cadre was that these party operatives be thoroughly versed in the political and ideological agenda of the ANC; it is in this document that the idea of establishing a 'political school' was first mooted. As broadly encompassing as this early profile was, it was also evident that the cadre functioned in difficult circumstances for a banned political organisation. In short, the importance of centralised accountability, functional performance and maintenance of discipline represented more than simply administrative necessities; they were also survival strategies.

The ANC's assumption of power in 1994 prompted the party to revisit and reorient its cadre policy, which was reintroduced officially at the party's 1997 national conference in Mafikeng. The significance of the Mafikeng interpretation of a cadre is of course that the party's own organisational circumstances had changed dramatically: from being a banned movement, it had been legalised and charged with forming the government. The reorientation of the cadre policy had come about because of 'the need to deploy cadres to various organs of the state, including the public service and to other centres of power in society'.[5] At the same time, in revisiting the policy the party retained some of the essential attributes that had defined a cadre at its Kabwe conference, including 'discipline, humility, modesty, a commitment to serve the people'.[6] What was significant about the Mafikeng policy reorientation was that 'deployment', which was one of several organising principles of a cadre's work at Kabwe, now seemed to take on a greater level of importance and urgency in circumstances that required the ANC to graft its organisational principles onto the state apparatus. The party resolved to 'put in place a deployment strategy which focuses on the short, medium and long term challenges, identifying the key centres of power and transform these centres'.[7]

The prioritisation of deployment in the wake of the ANC's accession to power was not only a practical necessity, but was also tied to the project of state 'transformation'. The state apparatus that the ANC inherited had served as a repressive machine which threatened the ANC's own existence just years earlier, and had comprised a racially unrepresentative body of officials highly politicised under years of National Party rule.[8] The policy corrective sought by the ANC was to transform employment demographically in state institutions to ensure greater representation of race and gender, especially at senior levels where blacks were historically marginalised. This also yielded strategic benefits for the ANC as a government in power, with the top echelons of the public service representing a key political power bloc.[9] Subsequent analysis has been more pointed, arguing that the ANC sought to forge a symbiotic relationship between state transformation through personnel changes and the extension of party control over the state: 'There is undoubtedly a confluence between these two definitions in that in order to achieve "transformation", the ANC argues it needs to strengthen its grip on the levers of power. Racial criteria have therefore facilitated, and are viewed as providing legitimacy for, the appointment of ANC members to key positions in the state.'[10]

If this was the stated aim of the party as it assumed the reins of government, the content of the new policy being written to transform the state machinery was more subtle in describing how personnel transformation should be effected. For example, the White Paper on Affirmative Action in the Public Service[11] argued that achieving a broadly representative public administration was crucial to restoring its legitimacy and credibility in the eyes of the majority of South Africans. The White Paper also argued that individuals who were historically marginalised might be better placed to administer services to constituencies similarly marginalised. Moreover, the issue of 'merit' was also reinterpreted for the process of recruiting state officials. For example, the White Paper on Human Resource Management[12] noted that 'Selection criteria ... will be based on competencies rather than undue over-emphasis on academic qualifications. Merit must be defined within the context of employment equity.'

Attempts to distinguish the party's policy of deployment from state transformation imperatives were also, ironically, accompanied by early criticism of the effects of the policy. A Presidential Review Commission[13] to consider initial efforts to restructure the state bureaucracy conceded that it was not surprising that the new ANC leadership viewed the public service it had inherited with suspicion and immediately sought to control appointments to its senior ranks. However, the commission also pointed to the quality of candidates it was actually yielding, noting that 'some of those new appointees have not been able to offer much beyond political loyalty'. A more recent comparative study[14] of party appointments to state institutions in Ghana and South Africa has described the ANC as being 'extremely sensitive to allegations of incompetence and mismanagement', in seeking to explain why control of state appointments did not appear to be greater in single-party dominant systems such as South Africa's in comparison to the more competitive Ghanaian case.

Nevertheless, through its cadre deployment strategy the ANC sought to gain considerably from the opportunities presented by state transformation. For instance, the relationship between ANC ministers and the heads of government departments (directors-general or DGs) in the period covering the reintroduction of the party's cadre policy was described as having been conducted in a policy 'vacuum', which allowed DGs greater space to exercise 'policy leadership'.[15] Although this was ironically attributed to instances of friction between ministers and DGs, it was also consonant with a policy of deploying cadres in the state with the expectation, stretching back to Kabwe, that each individual should be soundly versed in the party's political and ideological positions. A more direct manifestation of deployment has been observed by Cameron,[16] who distinguished between different 'waves' of party appointees. He argued that the second wave, marked by the introduction of the cadre policy in 1997, was more overtly political in its preference for party functionaries in comparison with the diversity of first-wave appointees, who shared an ideological consonance with the party's policy agenda. He added that this had a detrimental effect on 'management' capacity, a quality second-wave deployees lacked, though he cautioned that 'differences between the first and second wave appointees were not always watertight'.

Maphunye's analysis of politicisation among senior public servants sought to assess the effects of deployment from a sample of 180 interviews with middle-level and senior bureaucrats in two provincial departments[17] across four provincial governments and two national departments between 1999 and 2001. His research confirmed the discretion and sensitivity of the process – linked to a sense of the possible effects on administrative capacity – as well as a janus-faced quality in the policy's implementation:

> While not openly admitting that the party had deployed them, very few senior public servants boldy stated that in the present democratisation stage in South Africa the country could not afford to have a politically neutral public service. Overall, there seemed to be a quite wide belief that the top three positions of Chief Director, Deputy DG, and DG inevitably would be highly

politicised positions ... Some even suggested that deployment and re-deployment should begin at the lowest levels of the senior managerial ranks.[18]

Other evidence pointing to the scale and effects of the ANC's deployment strategy came from research conducted by state institutions themselves. That such evidence is mostly implicit and unclear shows once again how difficult it is to separate the aims of party policy from state transformation objectives. For example, the Public Service Commission (PSC), a statutory body, has on at least two occasions examined the turnover rate of heads of department in the public service. In its first study, published in 2008, there were several references made to 'deployment', although none was explicitly tied to the ANC's use of the term, as opposed to the generic allocation of scarce staff across the public sector depending on need.[19] This was also evident in a report on the state of public sector transformation produced by the Department of Public Service and Administration,[20] in which there was repeated use of the term 'deployment', as well as 're-deployment' and 'deployability', although this was again not directly or explicitly tied to ANC policy but to the mobility and rotation of senior public servants in the context of enhancing state capacity. Despite this, a wider historical contextualisation of the use of the term cannot reasonably dissociate it from its party guise, especially when applied to sensitive senior posts in the bureaucracy.

This is apparent elsewhere in the PSC's research on the turnover of departmental heads, which, despite the obscurity surrounding the use of the term 'deployment', made the more revealing observation that contract termination was the single biggest reason (59 per cent) behind the departure of heads in the period between 2003/4–2006/7; and, more revealing still, that as many as 89 per cent of current heads interviewed[21] believed that their tenure was directly linked to their relationship with ministers, or (essentially) party principals.[22] When read with another finding that 61 per cent of current heads believed that a change in minister would precipitate a change in their positions,[23] this suggests that deployment cannot simply be interpreted as an administrative act but must also be seen as a practice sensitive to changes in political oversight regulated by the ruling party. The PSC[24] produced a subsequent report on the turnover rate of departmental heads as occurring 'each time changes are anticipated at the political leadership level due to national and provincial elections'. The commission found a high level (43 per cent) of vacant posts towards the end of 2009 among national departments; while the vacancy rate varied at the provincial level, although only three of South Africa's nine provincial governments had rates in single digits. Potentially more telling was that the terms 'deployed' and 'redeployed' were explicitly used when describing many instances of mobility, especially at the provincial level.

The most explicit account of the effects of party-influenced deployment has been observed at the local level of the state. Cameron's[25] analysis, drawing on a variety of individual research, and corroborated by central government reports, links instability in the staffing of local government bureaucracies to clientelistic struggles over deployment wrought by localised ANC factionalism. Kopecký's[26] comparative study of party control of appointments in Ghana and South Africa seems to confirm the clientelistic nature of deployment practices in local government as described by Cameron. When asked what motivated party control of appointments, 'respondents also pointed out that jobs as rewards are quite often handed out in regional and local administrative units', compared with institutions at a national level. The ANC itself has recognised the scale of the problem and the potential risk it presents, given the institutional size and complexity of local government coupled with increasingly resitive local constituencies demanding better service delivery. The party introduced amendments to local government legislation in 2011 which sought to prohibit top municipal bureaucrats from holding office in a political party in any capacity.[27]

Deployment under attack and the challenges of party control

As a principle and practice, deployment as an instrument of state transformation has elicited polarising views, which provide insight into how the ANC has managed its own organisational transition. On the one hand, deployment as a means of extending the party's control over state institutions is considered 'undemocratic' and 'unconstitutional', in that it subverts the integrity of institutional checks and also feeds a process of 'centralization and elite control'.[28] Giliomee, Myburgh and Schlemmer[29] also express concerns with the practice, arguing that cadre deployment amounts to a bifurcation of state authority, with the result that real authority cannot be said to reside in constitutionally regulated structures (including the executive and parliament), but in party structures.

At the other end of the pole, Daniel Plaatjies[30] describes deployment 'as a mechanism to capture the state', but, in contrast to its critics, sees it as part and parcel of a globally accepted practice of politicisation, in which parties routinely attempt to exercise democratic accountability over unelected state institutions through appointments.

The polarisation of views should not obscure more nuanced observations of deployment in action. William Gumede, commenting in the context of an appraisal of governance arrangements in state-owned enterprises (SOEs) in South Africa, remarks: 'The one real danger is that the deployment strategy may undermine South Africa's formal constitutional lines of accountability and governance arrangements – and introduce an informal parallel and competing governance and accountability system.'[31] The notion of deployment as introducing a parallel accountability system in one sense clearly meshes with the view that deployment subverts constitutional process. But the context in which Gumede makes this comment, following a reference to the ANC's own criticism that party principals in government, such as ministers, have failed to consult party deployment structures prior to making senior appointments to SOEs, indicates that the integrity of the parallel and competing party system of vetting potential appointees to state institutions has itself come under pressure. This raises the question of whether the party has in reality been able to maintain centralised control over the deployment process, as its critics claim.

Cracks in the centralised cohesion of deployment, or the party's ability to maintain discipline over the process, have been explicitly and obliquely conceded. For instance, Seepe[32] remarks that 'with state power, the ANC has access to other forms of power', that is, other than its power rooted in 'the people'. 'The organisation has deployed its cadres to lead the state's ... apparatus. In such a power dynamic, unity in action cannot be assumed in the context of a liberation movement that has ascended the throne.' Seepe's primary point is that having made the transition to a governing organisation, the ANC runs the risk of substituting the power it derives from those it professes to serve ('the people') for that of the state machinery.[33] It is tempting to interpret his reference to 'unity of action' as not just applying to the party–people relationship, but also to the party's ability to exercise internal discipline over its deployment process.

More explicit concerns about a lack of unity in the party's attempt to control deployment through a hierarchy of centralised structures have been uttered by party principals themselves. Sheehan[34] cites an interview with ANC member and deputy minister Jeremy Cronin, who stated that 'the "deployment" of ANC notables into important positions in business and public institutions has simply caused a "multiplicity of centres of influence and power within the ANC", rather than the extension of a centralised authority'. The effects of this disunity were remarked on by the party's secretary-general, Gwede Mantashe, who conceded that 'mistakes [had been] committed by our structures in deploying cadres who do not even meet the basic requirements for the posts they are deployed in'.[35]

In her review of the evolution of deployment structures in the ANC, Booysen[36] explains that after the integrity of the party's National Deployment Committee (NDC) was questioned in 2001, the function of deployment became 'diffused' within the party organisation itself, or effectively carried out by its members within core operational structures or committees. This ironically represents the emergence of parallel and competing deployment structures *within* the party.

Concerns about deployment came to a head at the party's 51st national conference held in 2002 in Stellenbosch. This gathering also provided the best indication to date of how the party had managed the transition from non-state opposition actor to state governing organisation, having then completed a full five-year term (1994–1999). The secretary-general's report conceded that the party's accession to government had in fact unleashed some of the problems anticipated as far back as Kabwe, notably favouritism and opportunism. It noted that 'new opportunities for material and social advancement through positions in the public and private sector ... the availability of much greater choice of career paths ... the occupation of positions of power' could give rise to complacency, 'social distance' and careerism among deployees.[37] The sub-text of this statement acknowledged the strains placed on the party organisation's ability to centrally orchestrate the process and exercise accountability. The ANC resolved that its National Executive Committee (NEC) should be tasked with providing 'political direction to cadres deployed in all spheres of governance and to ensure accountability', including a 'mechanism' to evaluate the performance of deployees.[38]

Resolutions at the party's subsequent five-yearly conferences have reaffirmed this theme. The 2007 Polokwane conference resolutions instructed the party's NEC to strengthen 'collective decision-making and consultation on deployment of cadres to senior positions of authority', and gave the previously discredited NDC a new lease on life. It further resolved to improve the relationship and coordination between party structures and deployed cadres in the state.[39] The party's appeal to cohesion among its ranks would soon be tested after Polokwane in the aftermath of the removal from office of President Thabo Mbeki in 2008. The former DG in the Presidency, Frank Chikane, recalled the pressure that was brought to bear on caretaker President Kgalema Motlanthe to suspend decisions on the contract status of directors-general until after the 2009 elections, even though such contracts were not, at least formally, meant to be tied to the terms of those serving in elected office:

> This, of course, did not endear Motlanthe to some quarters within the ANC, who called for a moratorium on the

> appointment of new directors-general and other senior officials ... The moratorium ... must include the extension of contracts ... Interestingly, these positions were never translated into the official position of the ANC ... Every appointment or renewal of a director-general's contract was seen as an act of defiance against the positions of the 'party'.[40]

Finally, the most recent ANC conference in Mangaung in 2012 offered the most concrete response yet to the call made at its 2002 gathering to improve the coordination of deployment decisions. It proposed to do this by aligning deployment more directly to other pillars of its cadre policy going back to Kabwe, such as how cadres are recruited, educated and trained, and kept in check or held accountable: 'deployment should always be preceded by systematic academic, ideological, and ethical training and political preparation. Cadre deployment should be underpinned by a rigorous system of monitoring and evaluation of the performance of cadres.'[41] It is noteworthy that the document does not give further details on how a more rigorous system of monitoring and evaluation would look and function in practice, although it is more explicit about how to improve the training and political preparation of cadres by resurrecting the idea of a party 'political school', which has since been taken forward.

Conceptualising deployment in the context of party transition and state reconstruction

The discussion in this chapter questions how deployment should be understood conceptually, both in a broad comparative sense and in narrower contextual terms. In one vein, following Plaatjies, deployment can be likened to what public administration scholars have referred to as 'politicisation', or a generally accepted historical practice of exerting political control over career bureaucracies, which has evolved in a transparent and regulated manner to reflect a degree of mutual accommodation between political parties and career bureaucracies.[42] Peters and Pierre's[43] general definition of politicisation generally accords with the act of deploying party associates in state institutions through the 'substitution of political criteria for merit-based criteria in the selection, retention, promotion rewards, and disciplining of members of the public service'. Although it may be questioned whether this amounts in practice to a complete substitution or a partial one – recognising the fact that political and merit characteristics can coexist[44] – the point relates to the elevation in importance of party political reliability in the staffing of state institutions. This was certainly the formal aim of the ANC's deployment strategy after 1994.

Although the aim of deployment aligns with the concept of politicisation, deployment in South Africa is not otherwise consistent with the level of transparent and regulated accommodation of the practice as found in other state systems. For instance, I have argued elsewhere[45] that the statutory framework sanctioning politicisation in South Africa is, if not intentionally then unwittingly, ambiguous about what and who constitutes a political appointee in the state system, and at what levels discretionary appointments by parties are meant to apply. This corresponds with the less overt implementation of the ANC's deployment policy as advanced earlier. It also seems to accord with Kopecký's[46] statement that although most appointments to the bureaucracy in South Africa and Ghana are meant to be regulated by civil service legislation, 'in practice, parties in both countries have managed *to find loopholes in procedures* [my emphasis] and consequently have discovered ways to politicise appointments ... to a much larger extent than the law permits'.

On the one hand, this may suit the interests of the ANC, given that deployment represents, at a level of strategic agenda setting, an emphatic and unapologetic attempt by the party to colonise the offices of state institutions in order to leverage its exercise of political power. On the other hand, through signalling an appreciation for the need to build a professional bureaucracy, the party has in principle endorsed a proposal to introduce greater regulation of bureaucratic appointments at senior levels through reforms outlined in the National Development Plan,[47] which would essentially mean that such appointments are not made at the sole discretion of party principals in government. Indeed, a hitherto generally unregulated practice (with the exception of amendments to local government legislation), although beneficial for oiling the wheels of deployment, can also be a double-edged sword, by testing the party's ability to maintain centralised control and discipline over the process, which is diffuse, prone to instability, and can be mediated by the tactics of party principals.

It can also be argued that deployment conforms to the concept of 'patronage', defined as the ability or power of a political party to appoint people (its members or others) to positions in the public sector.[48] Patronage in this narrower interpretation overlaps with descriptions of politicisation, although the term becomes value-laden when interpreted more broadly to encompass clientelistic transactions or enabling corruption (quid pro quo particularistic exchanges),[49] elements of which have been linked to the practice of deployment at local government level. Kopecký[50] recognises this, noting that 'though distinct, patronage is a necessary condition for both clientilism and corruption', while at the same time advancing the point that patronage, as with politicisation, may also be motivated by parties seeking to exert policy control through state institutions. It is this interpretation of patronage that Kopecký finds prominent in his comparative study of Ghana and South Africa; where asked a question about the motivations of parties to appoint people to state institutions, most respondents[51] in both countries cited institutional 'control', followed by a mixture of 'reward' and control, and finally 'reward'.

Interpreting his findings across different types of institutions leads Kopecký to a more nuanced appraisal of the ANC's use of deployment as a tool of patronage. He argues that the party's policy in respect of new appointments in selected policy areas such as the economy, finance and foreign affairs has 'shifted' towards a greater emphasis on professionalism rather than ideological and partisan factors.[52] Booysen's[53] account of bureaucratic instability during the Mbeki–Zuma transition paints a less sanguine (albeit more general) picture of deployment politics. This also coincides with Chikane's recollection of the period, which refers to uncertainty and unease among sitting bureaucrats about the incoming cohort of ANC political principals among whom clientelistic pressures appeared more prominent.

Conclusion

If the ANC has been sincere about its commitment to a disciplined performance- and policy-oriented process of deployment since Kabwe, then its assumption of state power has clearly unleashed threats to the integrity of that commitment. It may be said that the party's accession to power has overextended its ability to centrally orchestrate deployment to meet purely policy ends, as a consequence of the privileges that state power has brought, its institutional complexity as well as the interests and responsibilities of party principals. At the party's 2002 conference, the secretary-general of the ANC responded to concerns about the quality of the party's cadres by admitting that it had been 'difficult, post-1994, to get leaders who are deployed to government to play a role in political education'.[54] From the perspective of the interests of party principals, it may be more fruitful to ascribe weaknesses in the ANC's ability to wield state power through deployment to Southall's[55] critique of the 'dominant party' thesis which has been applied to the party. Instead of viewing the ANC as a dominant party in a pure sense, which includes the cultivation of a 'highly centralised and hierarchical state', Southall contends that the dominant party argument, if not incorrect, is overstated. The party's ability to centralise power and blur the boundaries between party and state has faced 'significant limits', in its use of deployment as well, for reasons that include the recognition that the party represents a 'broad church' of sectional interests.[56]

So, if it can be said that the party's grip on the deployment process has weakened since it assumed control of the state, the rational course of action for any party organisation is to attempt to rein in the process in order to preserve the integrity of its 'primary goal'. For the ANC, deployment post-1994 has always been directly tied to its ability to pursue its pre-eminent goal of bringing about a 'National Democratic Revolution' (NDR). It has therefore retained its strategic commitment to deployment while making tactical adaptations in response to weaknesses in its ability to control the process. Resurrecting the idea of establishing a 'political school'[57] to imbue a new generation of cadres with the party's revolutionary, ideological and strategic positions is essentially an attempt to reassert control over deployment and institute a gatekeeping function over the process. It may also be viewed as an attempt to curb clientelistic pressures through a renewed emphasis on policy doctrine[58] in order to preserve the integrity and relevance of the NDR, although much will depend on how the party decides to link political education with deployment decisions.

The story of the ANC's transition as a party of resistance to a party of government, and that of the reconstruction of the South African state, are intimately entwined yet also obscured by the practice of deployment. This presents limitations for a wider and deeper theorisation of the practice while also exposing the need for more empirical research on the issue. In particular, we need much more historically oriented research to document the party affiliations of senior civil servants and executives of state-owned enterprises since 1994, how these have changed both quantitatively and qualitatively, and what this might reveal about the relationship between the internal contestation of ideas (for instance, policy control) and the promotion of sectional interests.

9

The idea of organisational renewal in the African National Congress

Heidi Brooks Yung

In the run-up to its National Policy Conference at Mangaung in December 2012, the ANC released a series of discussion documents, one of which was entitled 'Organisational Renewal: Building the ANC as a Movement for Transformation and a Strategic Centre of Power'. While organisational review and self-assessment are not new to meetings of the ANC, the 2012 report is distinctive from previous reviews not only in marking a particular juncture in the movement's history, but in calling for the 'rebirth' of the ANC. This chapter provides an analysis of the ANC's Organisational Renewal document, drawing on some of its key themes and conceptual preoccupations, with particular reference to vanguardism, mass mobilisation and cadre development.[1] It focuses on the way in which historical claims and movement traditions are both revisited and reinvented for the purposes of present-day party renewal. It argues that while the document places welcome emphasis on reconnecting the movement with the people, the concurrent weight given to the resurrection of past traditions does not necessarily augur well for democracy.

Organisational review in the ANC

Since the advent of democracy in South Africa in 1994 the ANC has undertaken several forms of organisational review,[2] none of which has been blind to its weaknesses and challenges. A number of the organisational challenges highlighted by the ANC in its 2012 Organisational Renewal document, including cadre development, branch revitalisation and the need to increase popular mobilisation, are variations on those set out at its National General Conference in 2000 and National Consultative Conference in 2007.[3] In fact it was a resolution of the 2007 Consultative Conference which spurred the ANC's National Executive Committee to declare 'a period of renewal'.[4] This declaration reaffirmed 'the need to place organisational renewal at the centre of our work' in the run-up to the ANC's centenary.[5] Given that the 2012 Organisational Renewal document again addressed itself to the 'challenges since 1994', one could be forgiven for feeling that the ANC is stuck in a self-assessment groundhog day. Inaction on resolutions taken at previous conferences, and thus their reappearance at subsequent meetings of the ANC, warranted the caution issued by the Congress of South African Trade Unions (Cosatu) that the movement risks 'sounding like a broken record'.[6]

The 2012 document's central theme of replenishing the movement's connection with the people is not especially surprising. The 2007 report of the Commission on Organisational Renewal previously asserted that 'mass mobilisation and organisational work should be stated as the primary pillar'.[7] What distinguishes the 2012 document from earlier iterations of organisational review is both the level of risk it perceives to the values and character of the movement, and the extent of the efforts required to regenerate the ANC as a political vanguard. While in 2007 a more optimistic picture was painted of the ANC's ability to increase contact with the masses and sustain their mobilisation – albeit with identified inadequacies in cadre development[8] – at its centenary there is a greater sense of urgency in the need to overcome the weaknesses of its first two decades in power. In 2012 the frank admission was made that 'the pace of socio-economic change and social justice at the core of the ANC project is being questioned by the ANC's support base'.[9]

The review also highlights concerns within the ANC since coming to power about its capacity 'to effectively lead the state and wield state power to advance the cause of the revolution'.[10] While this unease may be linked partly to the prevailing global economic orthodoxy which curtails state intervention, there is a recognition that the ANC's 'own internal weaknesses' are compromising its 'capacity to play its vanguard role as the leader of the state and society'.[11] The resolutions of the Mangaung conference highlight the need for a return to 'mass-based transformative politics'.[12] In no uncertain terms, the organisational renewal calls for 'the rebirth of the ANC'.[13]

It is perhaps fitting that the historical weight of the centenary celebration and its significance as a moment for reflection influence the tone of the document. The occasion is cast as providing the ANC 'with an unprecedented opportunity to reflect on our past in order to draw strength and courage to usher the movement and our country onto a new path'.[14] In some respects the review is an honest and candid reflection of organisational weaknesses and shortcomings, and even goes so far as to make recommendations to ensure the ANC's survival when it is out of office.[15] Moreover, despite its proven electoral success, the document acknowledges that the movement has had difficulty responding to 'the new realities and challenges' of coming to power.[16] As such, it contends that 'the ANC is nowhere near its aspiration of becoming the strategic centre of power'.[17] Cosatu's published response to the paper was equally frank: 'we must admit that we are a sick movement that fast resembles only a shadow of what it used to be'.[18]

It is worth considering to what extent the vulnerabilities in the ANC's mass character are being tackled as a result of its 2007 leadership change. After the replacement of Thabo Mbeki by Jacob Zuma as president of the ANC and of South Africa, Mbeki's aloof leadership style was juxtaposed with Zuma's man-of-the-people persona and popular support base.[19] The shutting down of critical voices and decline in the Alliance partners' influence became oft-cited features of the ANC under Mbeki. In general, however, the past record of the movement's organisational review, along with the cumulative nature of many problems facing the ANC, points to challenges that cannot be easily personalised. The more recent decline in Zuma's popularity, and the intriguing resurrection of the political figure of Mbeki by some sections of the ANC, also reflect the inadequacy of solutions rooted in a personalised politics. Nonetheless, it is possible to argue that Zuma's leadership has influenced the push towards reconnecting with the masses.

Renewal and the use of historical claims

Before we examine the themes which give effect to the renewal project, it is worth reflecting briefly on the significance of renewal itself. Although one might be accused of quibbling over semantics, it is significant to note that the ANC has referred to a project of 'renewal' as opposed to 'reform'. Renewal itself implies giving a new lease of life or strength to the movement — reflected also in references to 'rebirth' and 'replenishment'.[20] The combination of injecting the new while drawing on the past also implies some form of restoration and repair rather than the wholesale change or replacement that could be implied in 'reform'.

The ANC's is also not a project of modernisation per se. While its renewal proposals include recommendations related to information and communication technology and financial sustainability (neither of which is the focus of this paper), both areas of intervention are subject to the overriding imperative of a broader 'renewal' agenda. The flavour of the document is largely a call to past successes and draws predominantly on the ANC's identity as liberation movement, rather than as political party. Incumbency, along with the global context of neoliberalism, is in fact held liable for creating a number of the dangers that have faced the ANC since 1994, including social distance, corruption and intra-party factionalism.[21] Just as the movement made a call at the watershed moment of transition in 1994 for 'renewal and innovation' while 'building on [its] ... national liberation traditions',[22] so too does it call for the same at its watershed 'second phase of transition'.[23]

It is not uncharacteristic of the ANC to presage its texts and publications with a historical pre-amble. Indeed, discussion and policy documents, statements and other commentary often reflect on movement history. What is noteworthy about the organisational renewal presented at its centenary, however, is the combination of drawing on the movement's past to renew itself in the present. In this sense it is a twofold approach; of 'continuity in change'.[24] Proposals are structured around present challenges, but the document's tone is one of nostalgia.

Overall, the proposals for organisational renewal draw upon three interrelated areas of weakness: the challenges of government and political management of state power; internal movement stability; and organisational capabilities.[25] The document also draws on three 'conditions for renewal' centred on 'a resilient, courageous, principled and decisive leadership; a committed and conscious cadreship; and an active civil society and mobilised population'.[26] We can thus connect these requirements for renewal to three prominent themes: the role of vanguard leadership; the importance of cadre development; and the revival of the mass pillar.

Reviving the mass pillar

As a mass party, the ANC's longstanding connection with the people is a fundamental source of its strength and identity. This bond between movement and masses is credited by the ANC as being 'the single most decisive factor that brought about the 1994 democratic breakthrough'.[27] As such, the movement has asserted the continuing relevance of the struggle-era maxim 'the people are their own liberators'.[28] As Booysen has noted, however, this connection between the ANC and the people was stronger in 1994.[29] Reflecting on the rise in social protests, and sometimes heavy-handed response of the police, Southall also comments on the 'weakening of the bonds between the ANC and its historic community of support'.[30] Importantly, this trend has not gone unnoticed by the movement itself and in fact forms an important basis for the organisational reflections and resolutions of its centenary conference.

The section of the Organisational Renewal document that draws on 'lessons from our history' sets out the various points at which the ANC has undergone strategic and organisational change in response to conditions of the time. In doing so, it highlights the ANC's turn to mass mobilisation in the 1950s and the reaffirmation of its centrality in both 1969 (at the Morogoro conference) and in the transition from 1990 to 1993.[31] There is acknowledgement, however, that in the aftermath of 1994 'transformation of the state became the main pre-occupation of the organisation'.[32] The document therefore underscores mass mobilisation as a renewed priority for the next ten years.

A particularly noteworthy point is that the territory of 'mass mobilisation' is understood by the ANC as being at risk of occupation, not so much by opposition parties, as by formations from within the Alliance and Mass Democratic Movement (MDM) themselves. In seeking to strengthen the mass pillar, the ANC thus focuses on their renewal.

The Alliance, the MDM and renewal

In understanding its relationship with the masses, the document acknowledges the historical role of the revolutionary alliance between the ANC, South African Communist Party and Cosatu, confronting the question of how it relates to the governance process. In the process, it recognises the emergence of two competing tendencies: between the ANC as 'strategic centre of power and ultimate authority' and the Alliance as 'political centre'.[33] Yet beyond affirming the ongoing validity of the Alliance arrangement and the need for its involvement, it is not clear that this tension is resolved. The document emphasises that the Alliance is not a coalition and that the ANC must exercise power as the governing party. What is contended is that it must be the ANC that 'define[s] the parameters' of the Alliance partners' involvement in governance processes.[34] 'Skirmishes' between the trade unions and cadres in the state are recognised as putting a strain on the transformation project.[35] Yet it is notable that it is the structures of the democratic movement that are charged with relating to the democratic state 'as if it [is] their principal enemy'.[36]

While the ANC is critical of the 'statist' and 'bureaucratic' responses of its own cadres who seek to 'shut down rather than engage critical voices', its accompanying criticism that popular structures have failed to move from 'an oppositional posture' towards building 'transformative partnerships'[37] betrays an intolerance of alternative positions within its own camp. Cosatu's response to the document in fact registers its concern that 'anybody who disagrees may be labelled oppositionist'.[38] Thus while the ANC employs the characteristics of its struggle heritage, it is not too keen for civil society to do likewise by emulating past traditions of anti-state action and protest. For the ANC, the relationship between the democratic state and the trade union movement 'needs to be more transformative than oppositional'.[39]

A related concern regarding community mobilisation is the presence of in-fighting and contestation within the ANC's own ranks, and between local ANC and Alliance leaders in particular.[40] The causes of factionalism and opportunism are in part attributed to 'adverse socio-economic realities'. Yet there is also recognition that the upsurge of popular protest is linked to the erosion of the ANC's 'movement character'.[41] This, it argues, is being replaced 'in favour of a narrow party machinery that pre-occupies itself only with the "business of governing"'.[42] It is apropos this point that the ANC recognises the need to strengthen its own branches and to link ANC grassroots structures 'organically' to the people.[43] Rather than pointing to 'weaknesses' in local government or local movement structures as such,[44] it relates more directly to the very bond between ANC and people, and to the replenishment of that relationship.

On the one hand, the ANC's proposals recognise the need to embed the movement in people's 'daily struggles for a better life' and to 'step up' its capacity to improve that quality of life.[45] Unsurprisingly, the return to the 'mass line' advocated in the document was well received by Cosatu.[46] But concrete proposals to strengthen that grassroots relationship are largely absent. The content of the 'transformative politics' it advocates is also left unclear, but what is suggested largely equates to extending and deepening the influence of the movement.

Bearing in mind the ANC's aspiration to embed itself among the people, it is logical that its proposals pertaining to organisational design emphasise 'movement-building as opposed to narrow organisation-building'.[47] Presumably a re-rooting of the ANC among civic structures today would enable it to discharge its 'vanguard' role and give 'political, moral and intellectual leadership' to the 'wide range of social forces' which it led previously.[48] The appeal to make the ANC presence felt among civil society formations is not a far cry from the calls to infiltrate and build its underground machinery among popular formations in the 1970s and 1980s. The ANC's 1985 conference in exile recommended that 'ANC cores', intended to play a guiding and strengthening role, be formed within democratic mass organisations.[49]

What a transformative politics also implies is the renewal of a past relationship. The document proposes reconciling the tension within its own ranks between those cadres now in the state and those with their roots in the traditions of the MDM and Alliance[50] through the injection of an ANC presence into civil society. It states that 'Our movement must always be at the centre of civil society groups and social movements that are genuinely taking up issues affecting the motive forces and give political and ideological leadership'.[51] 'Transformative politics' in this sense is something of a double-edged sword. On the one hand, it is represented as a valued political tradition that has been lost in the throes of transition. But at the same time, in its renewed form, transformative politics must be detached from the 'oppositional' characteristics of its past lest they be used against the movement now in government.

While previous conferences have made vague resolutions to strengthen relations with both the Alliance partners and civil society,[52] the 2012 Organisational Renewal proposals appear to be the first since 1994 in which the ANC has set out the intention to revive civil society-based structures in a way that implies a return to a past ANC–MDM relationship. The ANC has often affirmed its role in encouraging the formation of 'progressive' civil society and working within it,[53] but here there is a sense of regret at the loss of this mass quality: 'In the pre-1994 era, the ANC was very successful in carrying out organisational, political and ideological work among various sectors. This included initiating the process of establishing and building progressive organisations ... In the post-1994 period, we have been more successful in doing sectoral work only at election time ... Unless there is a dedicated machinery to interact with sectors dynamically ... we can lose touch with key sectors of society.'[54]

The discussion recognises that the movement's ability to organise and mobilise among key sectors is the source of its mass character, and asserts the need to 'undertake a strategic review of the current state and role of all the organisations and formations that were part of the mass democratic movement'.[55] Among the subsequent conference resolutions is a decision 'to build and revive structures of the mass democratic movement and progressive civil society'.[56]

It may be that this intention is welcomed by current and former activists of MDM structures, as well as those disillusioned after 1994 by the dissipation of the vision for a more radical form of democracy. But it is not yet clear that this resolution will bring more, or even deeper, democracy. There is the possibility that the ANC's proposals for the extension of its reach over civil society may stifle popular democratic debate rather than enhance it. It also fails to confront the debate so prominent among MDM activists in the early 1990s regarding their co-option versus autonomy. To what extent can they continue to play a watchdog role while bringing their influence to bear on ANC thinking? What type of structures will provide for the input of these revived MDM formations, and on whose terms will their participation in the transformative agenda take place? To what extent will such forums build consensus or provide for difference among participants? The ANC's organisational renewal proposals leave much of this unanswered. What they imply is that today's challenges should be addressed through the revival of yesterday's organisations and allegiances. Historic sectors and communities of struggle are envisaged as having a new transformative role to play, yet while this takes us to a time gone by, it is not clear that this will mean a step forward.

The document is also noteworthy for the limited attention it directs to the mobilisation of new generations of young people and to the emergence of new interest groups and socio-economic differences within the African population itself. While it faces up to organisational challenges and weaknesses brought about by changed conditions, it lacks conceptual reflection on those changed conditions themselves. This lack of focus on the future is in fitting with its historical reflection. The ANC continues to adhere to the concept of national democratic revolution (NDR). Emanating from the thesis of colonialism of a special type, national democracy was originally envisaged as a necessary transitional stage that would achieve political democracy while paving the way for socialism. Since 1994 the concept of national democracy has become increasingly ambiguous, while any and all policies of the movement are projected as a fulfilment of the NDR.[57]

The call to replenish former connections and regenerate past attachments corresponds to the movement's theoretical and ideological lineage as well as its historical modus operandi. In calling for the strengthening of its broad church character, the ANC is playing to its historical strengths. The revival of these past characteristics is, however, taking place under different conditions. Although there is some acknowledgement of the need to mobilise 'the new social forces born out of our democracy', as well as the motive forces,[58] there is no analysis of the potential for difference and contradiction between and within these groupings. Their combination presupposes a policy agenda capable of uniting multiple forces and of representing all their interests (which presumably converge neatly under the NDR). Yet it cannot be assumed that sectoral interests can be 'aggregated' into common interests, as they have been in the past.[59]

Development activism and participatory democracy

In line with the mandate on movement-building, the Organisational Renewal proposals include a section on 'strengthening grassroots development-activism and participatory democracy'.[60] While the ANC has in the past emphasised the developmental role of both its own structures and those of its partners, particular space is given in the 2012 report to elaborating the term 'development activism'. In addition to the ANC branch becoming a 'strategic centre' for 'transformative politics in communities', the idea of development activism is contrasted directly with the 'oppositional politics of yesteryear'.[61] Through it, the ANC seeks to carve out a new space for action and partnership in transformation which targets the movement's identified areas of weakness. This is advanced as an approach to development that is neither 'statist' nor 'oppositional'.[62]

Development activism is also directly linked by the ANC to participatory democracy, 'broadly defined as an on-going process of empowering our people to play an active part in the processes that affect their lives'.[63] There is a longstanding belief in the ANC that democracy cannot be limited to features of procedural and electoral democracy alone. Pairing this with the danger of the masses becoming merely 'spectators' of governance,[64] the document contains a keen movement discourse promoting the principle of popular participation.

Reaffirmation of the role of participatory democracy in both the broader framework of South African democracy and the ANC's transformation project is certainly most welcome. However, it is not clear that the proposals will witness a strengthening of participatory institutions and practice. While the 2012 National Policy Conference discussion document on Legislature and Governance makes recommendations for strengthening community participation mechanisms in democratic local government, in particular the ward committee system,[65] the concept of 'development activism' in the organisational renewal report conflates popular input with leadership and representation by the ANC. It gives the gift of popular control in shaping development with one hand, but takes it away with the other by claiming that 'communities can shape the kind of development they want *if led by an agent for change* [emphasis added]'.[66] As the ANC understands itself to be the 'agent for change',[67] the participation of communities in shaping development is bound by their allegiance to the movement.

The document goes on to say that communities 'can also be misled by other forces contesting the space to turn against the ANC'. While this is conceded to be a result of 'social distance' and the ANC's 'absence on the ground',[68] the implication is that those who seek to shape development outside the movement framework are somehow non-transformative or merely misled. The recognition that people can contribute to transformation through other forces or representatives legitimately contesting that space is absent from the document, while references to participation do not suggest a role for citizen influence in decision-making itself. The link between local Alliance structures and the creation of strong participatory mechanisms is asserted both here and in earlier statements on local government. The former chairperson of the Provincial and Local Government Portfolio Committee Yunus Carrim remarked in 2001 that local government ward committees and ANC branches must be used to strengthen one another, and that 'ideally the ward committees should be used to mobilise the broadest range of interests in the community behind progressive goals as part of the overall national democratic transition'.[69] The inference is that community shaping of development is subject to movement imperatives or is somehow an intra-ANC activity.

An intriguing inclusion in the 2012 document is 'the creation of organs of people's power' as an element of organising and mobilising people for participation in transformation and development.[70] Organs of people's power became a feature of popular localised struggle in South Africa during the 1980s. Established by activists and civic organisations, these structures had roles that varied from providing advice and services to residents, to challenging the legitimacy of the local state and acting as forums for de facto self-governance and decision-making. Although the language of 'people's power' declined after 1990, its ethos has been credited with creating 'rudimentary principles' about participatory decision-making.[71] The organs of people's power were generally, however, ANC-aligned structures,[72] and accounts of the period have highlighted their sometimes coercive nature and political intolerance.[73] It is not clear from the Organisational Renewal document of 2012 what the ANC has in mind for 'organs of people's power'. The use of the term in the ANC lexicon has, in general, become somewhat diffuse in the post-1994 context. There is nonetheless the risk that such mechanisms for participation will be linked to the structures of the movement, rather than comprising multi-interest bodies for democratic participation.

Cadre development

A further theme prioritised in the renewal agenda is cadre development. Organisational emphasis on the requirements of building the ANC's cadreship is characteristic of the movement historically. The resolutions of the ANC's second national conference after coming to power declared the importance 'of having an army of conscious, committed and properly deployed cadres' to build the ANC.[74] Although succeeding conferences produced repeated agreement over proposals for cadre development, the 2007 report of the Commission on Organisational Renewal highlighted 'general impatience with lack of implementation'.[75] Taking up this challenge again, the resolutions of the ANC's 2012 conference placed 'the neglect of cadre policy ... at the centre of most of the current weaknesses and challenges faced by our movement in the post-1994 era'.[76] It thus recommends the decade 2012–22 be known as 'the decade of the cadre'.[77]

The strengthening of cadre policy and the elimination of the problem of factionalism are linked to the broader project required to safeguard the 'integrity' and 'core values' of the ANC.[78] In addition to building academic skills and raising literacy levels within its ranks, a key element of its cadre policy is political education and training.[79] In fitting with the document's historical reflection, cadre policy continues to be rooted in the ANC's past revolutionary character. Interestingly, a significant portion of the chapter is dedicated to reiterating the aspects of cadre policy and ideological work set out at the ANC's 1985 Kabwe conference. The document reaffirms the revolutionary role of its cadres and proposes the establishment of a programme 'to build a contingent of new cadres', focusing on ideological and academic training.[80] It also places renewed focus on the institutionalisation of such education through the establishment of an ANC political school.[81]

The document emphasises a commitment to the wholesale up-skilling of cadres, points to particular knowledge and competency requirements and addresses the importance of self-discipline, personal initiative and self-empowerment by cadres themselves in addressing both organisational and governance challenges.[82] The extent to which these pronouncements can generate implementation remains to be seen. What can be heard is a note of general lament that ideological and academic training has received insufficient attention. Given the renewed emphasis on the regeneration of leadership and the education of its cadres, it is perhaps worth noting the impact on the ANC of a new generation of cadres and members. The ANC's National General Conference in 2000, for instance, reflected on the pre-1994 period when it argued that cadres developed a level of theoretical understanding that led to 'common methodology' and 'discouraged opportunism and careerism'.[83] In 2007, however, the movement bemoaned the inadequate 'socialisation and politicisation' of new cadres entering the movement.[84] A generational shift within the ANC has led to the emergence of a new breed of cadres not schooled in ideology or theory, as their predecessors were.

It is therefore timeous that the Organisational Renewal document was launched shortly after a wave of indiscipline within the ANC, including the expulsion from the movement of Youth League president Julius Malema in February 2012. Although it is unfortunately not clear who was responsible for drafting the document, the renewal agenda, in general, seems to have received public backing from some of the ANC's Gauteng contingent, in particular ANC provincial secretary David Makhura,[85] who chaired the ANC's Organisational Renewal Commission and spoke at the document's launch in April 2012.[86] Gauteng ANC chair Paul Mashatile[87] and regional secretary-general Paul Mojapelo also expressed support for renewal and political education.[88] Then National Executive Committee member Febe Potgieter-Gqubule, who was on Malema's Disciplinary Committee,[89] also joined Makhura on the Organisational Renewal Commission.[90] Perhaps most notably, it was National Executive Committee member and former Youth League leader Fikile Mbalula who gave the presentation on Organisational Renewal at the 2012 National Policy Conference itself.[91] As he was a former political ally of Malema and was now firmly in the Zuma camp, one could speculate whether Mbalula's involvement was intended to send a warning to rebellious younger comrades. In an interview in June 2013 following the announcement of Malema's intention to establish a new rival party, the Economic Freedom Fighters, Mbalula accused his former comrade of both immaturity and impatience, adding that 'Julius's generation had not had that opportunity to get political education'.[92]

Given that ANC leaders and members themselves act as 'agents for change',[93] cadre policy is a key function of the movement's strength. It thus seems likely that it was growing concern within the ANC to regain control of its younger, more maverick cadres that led to the proposals to introduce greater discipline and training with a focus on political education.[94] In the renewal document, earlier traditions of the recruitment and development of revolutionary cadres by the Communist Party and ANC are spoken of with admiration, while the movement's shortfalls in respect of key elements of its cadre policy adopted in exile are set out in turn.[95] The role assigned to the ANC political school system makes, however, for a somewhat instrumental conception of its cadreship. The document envisages that the schools 'will massively churn out the cadres who are properly prepared for the tasks of revolutionary transformation of our society'.[96] Its discourse in a sense reproduces the historically teleological role of masses and cadres. Indeed, it is notable that inspiration for the school seems to have emerged from the Communist Party of China's leadership academy.[97]

While the emphasis may be on education, the accompanying imagery is of a giant machine moulding and producing in vast numbers disciplined revolutionaries to the required spec. After the launch of the renewal document, SABC political analyst Ralph Mathekga argued that 'discipline' was not the answer to the movement's internal challenges. He instead suggested that the ANC ask itself 'how the party can adopt the necessary internal institutional changes to accommodate the new breed of membership'. He went on to comment: 'The reason why the party continues to experience internal tensions that manifest themselves as poor discipline is because ... [it] ... has not adopted the institutional mechanisms to allow for a free flow of ideas within the party ... To arrive at the envisaged level of discipline expressed in the discussion documents, the party would have to shut down debates altogether.'[98]

An important nuance in this discourse is the distinction that seems to be made between the ANC's 'members' and its 'cadres'. The resolutions of the 2012 National Policy Conference stressed that 'ANC members should understand fully what it means for a member to go through the full cycle of becoming and remaining a tried and tested cadre. It must be clear that joining the ANC is the beginning of a long journey towards becoming a cadre.'[99] In respect of membership, the Organisational Renewal document refers to the need to introduce a more 'rigorous' political induction process and states that new members must undergo political education and be 'active in community and sectoral organisations'.[100] However, cadreship, which occupies a full chapter of the document, appears to be a more distinct classification. Interestingly, although there is valuable emphasis on improving literacy and the provision of general education for cadres,[101] both the role of the ANC's political school in 'churning out' cadres and the disciplinary requirements of cadreship itself raise the question whether critical debate is being encouraged or ideological and revolutionary conformity preferred.

The people and the vanguard

It is not the purpose of this chapter to analyse the applicability to the ANC of the 'mass party' typology. However, a few words are worth saying about the state of the ANC as a mass party (or movement) in so far as this identity pertains to its renewal agenda. Darraq argues that while the ANC's mass character has been eroded since the assumption of office, it still retains many of its mass features.[102] In terms of the mass party typology originally theorised by Maurice Duverger, the ANC draws its strength and very *raison d'être* from its membership, as well as placing importance on the recruitment and political education of members.[103] Booysen has observed that the ANC doubles up as a ruling party and popular movement,[104] and it is the bridging of these two roles that gives the party its continued mass character. Yet in assuming this dual identity, the ANC also embodies a complexity of characteristics and traditions for which a purely organisational typology cannot necessarily account or explain.[105]

Although the ANC continues to appeal to its mass character and heritage, its Organisational Renewal document reflects the very challenges it faces in retaining roots in communities while also assuming the mantle of state power. By its own admission the ANC has struggled to straddle the roles of both liberation movement and ruling party.[106] Its continued use of revolutionary and insurrectionary language in a framework of liberal democracy[107] also reflects the sometimes uneasy pairing of this dual identity. The ANC today is thus necessarily born of its past. Its relationship with the people as both a movement and a party must therefore be understood through the lens of historical struggle as well as ideological tradition. The use of historical claims in its renewal agenda derive from this heritage. Importantly, its identity is not only one of a liberation movement and ruling party but also a political vanguard of the people.

The self-application of the status of vanguard highlights the continued relevance of the ANC fulfilling its historical role to sustain mass political consciousness and self-organisation toward the goal of NDR. With this in mind, the recognition that the space of mass mobilisation has been left open to alternative forces[108] indicates the presence of a threat to that vanguard status and to its revolutionary objectives. The status of the people's vanguard, in particular in a pluralistic democratic context, is essentially a tenuous one. It is only earned by virtue of being recognised as such by the people themselves. Just as in a traditional socialist vanguard party, the revolution cannot take place purely from above. Rather, the people must be convinced of the need for revolutionary transformation, and the vanguard movement must secure their support for and active participation in that objective.[109]

As a movement in public office, despite attempts to institutionalise popular participation, the ANC admits that 'it has not mastered the art of combining state power and mass power'.[110] This additional dimension of vanguardism must be accounted for in the analysis of its party-movement identity. The vanguard role reflects the ANC's dominant roots in both African nationalism and Marxism-Leninism. It is this heritage which helps to explain the movement's display of certain features reminiscent of a vanguard-type party, while also aspiring to retain the broad 'united front' politics of a movement.[111]

The tension in this dual role is also visible in the cadre–member relationship. During its time as a banned movement, the role of cadres was critical in bringing the movement to the people in a context in which membership was illegal. The ANC's underground cadres fulfilled a vanguard role. The pressures and restrictions of exile and illegality also forced on the ANC a mode of organisation more akin to a traditional Leninist party, with a cell structure and centrally controlled corps of cadres, albeit with a broad church programme.[112] Since the ANC's unbanning, and in fitting with the character of a mass party, the movement is clear that membership is open to all. At the same time, however, it has tended to retain the most experienced and disciplined of its cadres at the party centre and in key positions in public office. There is at once a desire to maintain a strong mass structure, connected to the grassroots, while simultaneously recruiting from this pool those who can best serve the movement. The prominence given to each of these elements in the Organisational Renewal document of 2012 suggests that achieving this dual objective continues to present a challenge.

Conclusion

Overall, the ANC's 2012 Organisational Renewal document combines an honest reflection on organisational shortcomings and challenges with a reflection on past successes. It is in the claims of the latter, rooted in its mass liberation movement identity, that the renewal agenda is rooted. This chapter has sought to show how the ANC draws on its historical traditions, identity and successes to inspire renewal in the present. It has also drawn out key themes in the report that centre on revival of the mass pillar, cadre development and the ANC's party-movement role as vanguard of the people.

Unsurprisingly, the proposals for renewal play to the ANC's historical strengths. The mass line approach and its broad church character remain indispensable to the movement's longevity. In contrast with previous reviews of the organisation, however, the 2012 document suggests a desire to return to an earlier point in time, requiring the rebirth of the vanguard movement and the replenishment of its connection with the masses. Restoration of internal party stability, cadre discipline and mass confidence in the ANC's transformative capacity are central to the renewal project.

The call for the rebirth of the movement is likely to appeal to activists and cadres of the ANC who have been disappointed by the shift to 'palace politics', and indeed those on the left who saw the change of leadership from Mbeki to Zuma as marking a shift in the locus of power from party centre to the people. It may be that the honesty of the account presented at Mangaung is a reflection of just this shift in focus. As Southall suggests, however, it is not clear that the ANC is prepared 'to move beyond radical rhetoric'.[113]

Moreover, the resurrection of historical modes of expression does not necessarily portend a more democratic connection with the people. Cosatu's call for greater prominence to be given to the mass-based national liberation movement character of the ANC[114] may well be a misplaced nostalgia. Many traditions well suited to the demands of struggle and people's power are not conducive to the context of a pluralistic democratic state and its accompanying institutions. The mass activity and mobilisation of the 1960s–1980s demanded unity and conformity, while structures of popular power were imbued with the common goal of defeating the apartheid state. In the post-1994 period, structures purporting to be mechanisms of a democratic state must be subject to democratic contestation. Their role cannot be tied to any one political organisation or preordained programme. The content of ANC proposals for the revival of its mass character suggests that certain dangers are implicit in the resurrection of the past. In extending the ANC's reach across civil society and merging participatory democracy with the strengthening of the movement, the possibility arises that its liberation movement heritage may undermine its role as a party in a democratic system.

The proof will emerge over the coming decade as the ANC implements the resolutions of its National Policy Conference. Many of the document's proposals on organisational renewal appear to have been accepted. Concerns about 'indiscipline' in the ANC remain, and the movement has already begun political education courses through the Walter Sisulu Leadership Academy.[115] The long-awaited political school itself still remains to be built.[116] We can also hope to see a reflection on progress made at the ANC's next policy conference in 2017. There should, however, be some note of caution. Even if the ANC makes progress in rebuilding its relationship with the masses and developing a cadreship able to root the movement in communities as well as extend its reach, we may well have a more active and mobilised movement, but not necessarily a more democratic one.

10
Which future for the African National Congress?

Anthony Butler

This book hopes to stimulate debate about the future of the ANC and, by extension, the future of South Africa's political system. One recent wide-ranging survey of the experiences of dominant parties concluded that 'with few exceptions, most ... former dominant parties survive their defeats'.[1] The chapters in the book explore just how dominant parties like the ANC can defer defeat and how parties that have lost power can come back and win again.

There are special lessons to be learned from parties that are in many respects like the ANC – dominant parties confronting the deep challenges posed by political life in middle-income developing countries. There is also potential wisdom to be gleaned from the study of quite different political parties, such as the Chinese Communist Party and Brazil's Workers' Party, about how party organisational and political challenges can be managed.

Even in the most difficult circumstances, a party is never locked into organisational degeneration. Party leaders are capable of self-conscious strategic renewal and so they are never inescapably trapped by their past or by a hostile environment. No party or liberation movement is destined to follow any particular pathway towards terminal decline.

Classic sociological analyses of the 'life cycles' of parties understandably focused on the emergence of oligarchic tendencies.[2] In more recent decades, scholars have emphasised how long-range adaptation to the external environment has made parties more 'catch-all' in character, or even integrated them into 'cartelised' political systems.[3] Such approaches have suggested that strategic adaptation is desperately difficult. Over the past two decades, there has also been increasing attention to shorter-range party adaptation and to the influence of party goals on such adaptation.[4] Recent theories of party change suggest that defeat, leadership turnover and factional realignment can improve a declining party's political prospects.

The cases considered in this book suggest that the substantive character of party adaptation spans a wide range of organisational, ideological, policy and political changes. None of the possibilities for party renewal and reconstitution is, of course, realised automatically or easily. Reform initiatives sometimes succeed and sometimes fail. It requires a combination of good political judgement and strong leadership – and also a measure of luck – for a struggling party to rebuild its political prospects.

This chapter explores some of the organisational and political challenges that currently confront the ANC. Drawing on the earlier chapters of this book, it then sets out some of the key dimensions of a potential reform or party rejuvenation project, and identifies the potential opportunities for, and obstacles to, ANC renewal.

What is wrong with the ANC?

The ANC is both old and relatively new. It was formed more than a hundred years ago as a representative body for regional African leaders confronting deepening white supremacy and racial exclusion. After spending much of the 20th century engaged in fruitless elite politics, or in the doldrums of exile, the ANC was re-created in 1990 in the form of a mass movement. Although the branch was ostensibly placed at the centre of the organisation's elective candidate selection and public policy choices, ANC leaders maintained central control by using a combination of procedural manipulation, patronage, co-option and invented tradition. This resulted in a tightly circumscribed internal democracy, central veto powers and relative organisational stability.[5]

Declining coherence

The ANC has found it increasingly hard to maintain its 'broad church' character and any pretence of ideological coherence. The deepest causes of conflict in the ANC result from changes in the class character of the organisation. Previously united by opposition to apartheid, the ANC now contains an affluent bourgeoisie, a significant 'new' middle class (with a particularly heavy representation of public-sector trade unionists), a traditional working class, in the mines, factories and service industries, and a broad base among the poor and economically marginalised. The different interests and perspectives of these classes are reflected in disputes about public policy. Such conflicts are no longer effectively managed by the ANC's tripartite alliance with the South African Communist Party and the Congress of South African Trade Unions, because these two bodies have themselves become embroiled in factional politics and are increasingly divided by the diverse interests and preoccupations of their own activists.

The unhappy result has been an ANC that has lost policy direction and cannot escape interminable internal conflict. Current efforts to bolster orthodox economic policy-making, to improve long-range planning, to privilege reason and evidence in policy deliberations and to subordinate particular interests to broader developmental imperatives depend upon recognition that South Africa is tied into an international capitalist order. The predominance of private property, and resource allocation primarily through markets, will continue to circumscribe policy options.

In today's ANC, however, many political activists now regard the conservative cast of economic and developmental policy as an ideological commitment rather than a pragmatic reflection of the economic constraints on modern politics. Their impatience is reflected in an avowedly more radical advocacy of public ownership and state-led development as keys to a fast-growing and more equal society. The outflanking of the ANC on the left by the Economic Freedom

Fighters (EFF) and elements in the trade unions poses a special challenge to ANC strategists.

Meanwhile, during its more than two decades in power, the ANC's organisational coherence has also eroded. Membership has grown from a little over 400 000 in 2002, to 600 000 in 2007, and then to 1.2 million in 2012.[6] Conference resolutions imply that this growth was partly planned: in 2007, for example, the ANC resolved to grow systematically across the country before the movement's centenary celebrations, taking 'steps to practically implement the target set by the 1942 Conference of 1 million members'. The objective of the ANC, according to current secretary-general Gwede Mantashe, has been to complement recruitment with 'intensive branch political education programmes to improve the quality of members'.[7] Mantashe's belief that a large membership is desirable may be inspired by the expansion of the Chinese Communist Party from 50 million members to more than 85 million. Mantashe claims the ANC needs 2.5 million members in order to be 'competitive' as electoral challenges arise.

The truth is, however, that the movement's remarkable membership growth has been driven mostly by subnational factors, and in particular by competition for office between party factions. This underlying political dynamic of factional competition has itself been propagated mostly by activists' pursuit of resources. The national leadership cannot easily bring the money-fuelled membership expansion to a halt: as Mantashe himself has observed, the ANC cannot 'deliberately stop people from joining it'.[8]

Occupation of public office has further undermined the ability of the ANC's leadership to impose party discipline upon activists. ANC policy documents pretend that the movement has been extending its control over the state, parastatals and big business, but the reality is very different. The apartheid state and economy have proven very durable, and they have absorbed much of the leadership of the ANC without their fundamental character being changed. At lower levels of the state, ANC offices have become stepping stones to public sector employment and to control over government tenders.[9] Internal ANC elections and candidate selection processes have become characterised by factional conflicts that are fuelled by private resources.[10] ANC intellectuals have identified further 'sins of incumbency' that have arisen as the unintended consequences of being a party of government, with access to state resources, for more than two decades.[11] Meanwhile, established business has drawn much of the new political elite into directorships and economic opportunities without any significant change being ceded in the structure or ownership of the economy.

Candidates and leaders

Many basic party functions, including candidate selection and leadership elections, have degenerated as a result of such trends. Secretary-general Gwede Mantashe informed the ANC's 2012 Mangaung conference about a senior task team's report on irregularities in the candidate selection process for the 2010 local government elections. Chaired by party stalwart Nkosazana Dlamini-Zuma, the team had been asked to investigate departures from the formal electoral guidelines and the manipulation of electoral processes.[12] Task-team members investigated the whole list process, exploring branch meetings, screening committees and public consultations in more than 400 wards. Widespread manipulation was uncovered: 'bulk membership' and 'gatekeeping' was found to be commonplace, and 'the observed trend' was 'that members are no more treated as important human beings'. Instead, the 'focus is more on … the buying of forms which can be given to anyone as they can be owned by those that have resources'.[13]

Parallel membership regimes were also widespread in which power-brokers hoarded and manipulated membership forms. The 'owners' of such forms used them to make quorate meetings impossible. Other abuses included boycotts, the creation of illicit structures, parallel meetings in different venues, and the improper exclusion of members from branch meetings.[14] The report painted a dismal picture of the state of ANC internal democracy. Real or ghost 'members' were used as instruments in competition for leadership positions.

These findings were echoed in a 2012 Constitutional Court

judgment. The court explored delegate selection processes at provincial level in response to a legal action brought by members of the Free State ANC. The appellants claimed that the ANC 'ignored and failed to investigate' alleged irregularities and that the provincial secretary 'deliberately turned a blind eye to these discrepancies, which were brought to its attention on numerous occasions'.[15] The claimants' material grievances concerned 'the question whether the delegates to the elective Provincial Conference had been properly accredited and audited as required by the ANC's constitution and its Membership Audit Guidelines'. The answer, according to the court, was that they had not.[16]

Delegates had not been 'duly mandated or elected' at properly constituted branch general meetings. Membership numbers were manipulated in branches, which allowed factional leaders 'to send delegates to the provincial conference or to send a different number of delegates than they would lawfully be entitled to'. The court also uncovered 'the exclusion of bona fide delegates who had been elected at properly constituted branch general meetings' and the exclusion of 'members in good standing from participating in the election of delegates'. All these infractions were worsened by leaders' sanctioning of the outcomes of these abuses of power and process.[17]

At national level, campaigns for leadership positions have resulted in further manipulation of membership systems and numbers. Competing factions push up audited membership numbers in regions and provinces in which they are popular, and in which they, or their factional allies, enjoy organisational control. Meanwhile, they try to minimise delegate numbers in areas controlled by their opponents and use procedural manipulation to disqualify members or branches whose loyalty is in question.[18]

In the late 1990s, when the dynamic of expanding membership began to unfold, it was the growth of Thabo Mbeki's home province – the Eastern Cape – that led the way. The provincial party was smaller than its KwaZulu-Natal (KZN) and Limpopo counterparts in 1997. By the end of Mbeki's first term as ANC president, however, Eastern Cape had leapfrogged its peers to become the biggest province by far. Other provinces also pursued membership growth. The provincial party in KZN was able to capitalise on the steady deterioration of the Inkatha Freedom Party (IFP) by expanding northwards. It also out-competed the IFP in burgeoning urban and peri-urban areas in the KZN south and Midlands.

At the 2007 Polokwane conference, Mbeki was ejected from the ANC presidency by a cross-national coalition bolstered by almost universal support, in KZN, for Jacob Zuma. As the 2012 Mangaung conference approached, membership numbers again started to rise rapidly in almost all provinces, and there were further reported instances of procedural manipulation by provincial and national office-holders. Provinces in which Zuma enjoyed less popularity, notably the Eastern, Western and Northern Cape, experienced falling accredited memberships. Of the 14 per cent of branches that did not qualify to send delegates to the Mangaung conference, most were anti-incumbency redoubts in the Eastern Cape and North West. Critics complained that the incumbent faction had used its bureaucratic power to manipulate accreditation and auditing processes.

As a result of the growth in membership, the challenges of party management have redoubled. A growing proportion of the ANC's membership comprises fresh recruits who have not internalised the movement's invented traditions and conventions of seniority and legitimate power. A further incalculable (but probably large) proportion of new members are essentially paper fictions or the pawns of party power-brokers.

Routine organisational systems

More routine organisational challenges confronting the ANC include a dependency on paper-based records, weak information and communications systems, and a failure to exploit information technologies and social media fully. Three times in every five years, as elective or candidate list processes begin again, the movement's dysfunctional internal systems hamper effective management of the party. The ANC is unable to perform the broader benign functions of a political party as effectively as it could. It cannot successfully give voice to popular discontent and it does not serve as a strong bridge between activist citizens and the national political elite. This may have encouraged citizens to embark upon more direct actions, including at times violent 'service delivery protests', to express their grievances.[19]

In discussion documents and conference resolutions concerning party reform in recent years, a project of 'renewal' has been proposed through which the alleged historical strengths of the ANC – discipline, deliberation and mass participation – might be reconstructed.[20] In Mantashe's eyes, 'empowering the branches … will ultimately save the movement'. The 2012 conference endorsed a new focus on organisational issues, announcing a 'decade of the cadre'. It remains unclear how much political capital will be thrown into this effort: activists will allegedly be subjected to 'performance monitoring'; 'firm and consistent action' will instil discipline; and 'integrity commissions' will purportedly improve the quality and character of deployees. Meanwhile, a 'comprehensive' political education system will begin to 'restore' the alleged character and knowledgeability of ordinary members.

Such backward-looking proposals for the recovery of past traditions have been accompanied by appeals for modernisation and the deployment of new technologies. Some basic administrative systems have been improved. Mantashe recently celebrated 'workshops to train branch representatives on the membership audit', which have apparently produced 'visible improvement in the keeping and maintenance of branch membership records'. The secretary-general has also identified ways to minimise membership gatekeeping by centralising membership card distribution, arguing that 'modern technology is not a luxury and there should not be any reluctance in investing in it'.[21] Such calls for technological innovation have been a feature of ANC politics since Thabo Mbeki's first term, though grassroots suspicion about the power it might place in the hands of incumbents remains widespread.

Procedural and constitutional changes have also been introduced. The 2012 conference adopted new rules about lobbying, the use of money in internal elections, and improper conduct in political meetings. The barring of simultaneous membership of more than one constitutional structure of the ANC has been designed to regulate the influence of provincial power-brokers in the political centre.[22] Recently some ANC leaders have returned to previous proposals for a permanent electoral commission to be established. In early 2012 Zuma condemned the internal electoral system from which he had himself benefited. The ANC, he asserted, needed to review its elections 'in order to enhance internal democracy, credibility of the process, as well as the integrity and suitability of candidates'. Such changes are necessary to 'protect the ANC from the tyranny of slates, factions and money'.[23]

Six considerations for party reformers

Rejuvenating an ailing party is never easy. Party leaders must address the complex and unique challenges that derive from a party's own history, culture and political environment. There are no reliable templates that can be borrowed from other parties — not even from organisations that share common experiences as dominant parties of government in developing countries, or from comrades who claim similar ideological or historical roots.

Adapting to change is, however, never something entirely new. After all, a dominant party, in order to stay dominant across two or more decades, must already have reacted repeatedly and self-consciously to assorted political challenges. When such a party's leaders are hit by the crisis of electoral defeat — or by the fear of its impending arrival — they find themselves with a bewildering range of potential options. To name but a few: they can undertake changes to their identity and ideas; refashion their programmes and public policies; remake party constitutions; modify procedures for selecting leaders and candidates; open up or close down intra-party democracy; renew, expand, contract or re-educate their memberships; subvert democratic institutions and practices; or repress their opponents, using their grasp of the levers of state power.

Party leaders, as we have emphasised, will approach organisational and political adaptation informed by their party's goals. But what do parties really want?[24] Their objectives are likely to include some mix of vote maximisation; the pursuit of office (or particular offices); the realisation of policy objectives; and a desire (on the part of activists at least) for internal party democracy to grow. In the self-conscious reflection about goals in the ANC's strategic documents, such objectives are mixed together with a broader pursuit of human emancipation and ideological hegemony.[25]

Dominant parties are likely to experience serious conflicts over party goals because they embrace such a wide range of constituencies and interests. They also deliberate upon the historic purposes of their movement using doctrinal formulations (such as 'national democratic revolution') that are deliberately opaque and accommodate diverse aspirations and philosophies. Bigger parties at least tend to be more consistently office-seeking and centrist in their behaviour than their smaller counterparts (and dominant parties are always big parties). For this reason, they are more likely to be pragmatic in their strategies for occupying the central space in politics.[26] Dominant parties are also long-term governing parties, and the objectives they pursue are shaped by their extended and intricate relationships with the state and with business. Beyond these broader considerations, the chapters in this book suggest that there are six key factors that reformers should bear in mind when contemplating a party reform project.

Firstly, don't panic. In dominant party systems, the opposition is almost always weaker than it appears. The ruling party has a reservoir of trust, patronage networks and skilled political activists at its disposal. Opposition parties find it hard to move to the centre-ground of politics and to secure sustainable popular support. Even in the realm of ideology, a dominant party's ideas continue to hold sway even after an electoral defeat and eviction from legislative and executive offices.[27]

Secondly, modernisation is inescapably political, and the implications of each administrative and procedural reform need to be carefully calculated. Changes to basic administrative systems; the introduction of new technologies to manage membership recruitment and retention;

mechanisms for running internal list processes and elections; and performance-monitoring systems: all of these can radically change who holds power in the party (usually to the benefit of the centre). So, too, can the introduction of mandatory 'political education' programmes and the development of difference classes or categories of membership or cadreship.

Thirdly, money is central to politics. The ability to channel resources, such as jobs and public services, to particular constituencies lies at the heart of many dominant parties' endurance in power. But patronage can alienate voters, and the power-brokers who mobilise voters in exchange for resources are a threat as well as a resource. Moreover, slow-growing and sclerotic economies such as South Africa's simply cannot sustain patronage relationships on a sufficient scale to sway electors. And money politics is at the heart of the factional struggles that have the power to tear a dominant party apart. The availability of public funding, transfers from parastatals, and private donations all have ambivalent effects. Distribution and openness matter: national control over financial resources, when combined with transparency legislation, can empower the centre of the party, limit the accumulation of 'war chests' at lower levels, and stabilise factional jostling for offices.

Fourthly, leaders in the centre must respond to the interests and perspectives of their party peripheries and regions. In middle-income countries, there are typically vast developmental and economic gulfs between urban and rural constituencies. A balance must be struck between centralisation and decentralisation when it comes to candidate selection, control over the distribution of state and party resources, and the selection of regional and national leaders. It is essential, in particular, to avert large-scale regional defections that can provide a platform for the growth of opposition challengers.

Fifthly, the character of factional politics in a dominant, or once-dominant, party is central to its prospects for success. 'Unity', as Boucek observes, 'is a necessary, albeit insufficient, condition for party dominance.'[28] Dominant parties need to maintain coalitions of voters, special groups and allied parties. But, above all, in order to avoid 'degenerative factionalism', they need to sustain a coalition of inevitably competitive internal factions. Boucek observes that 'the intra-party dimension of competition is a critical factor in explaining the maintenance and the decline of dominant parties'. We would add that it is crucial to understanding their resurgence.

Finally, the leaders of dominant parties threatened with defeat can embrace electoral competition, resist it or subvert it. Some members of each of the dominant parties explored in this volume espouse nationalist or quasi-socialist ideologies that can be used to justify the manipulation of electoral rules and institutions, to promote mobilisation around race, religion or ethnicity, to abuse freedom of the media and other political freedoms, and to subvert judicial independence. The conditions under which mild subversion becomes authoritarian repression are in part a product of deliberation among dominant party leaders and strategists.

The ANC is not set on any ineluctable path into the future. Our exploration of the experiences of other governing parties in middle-income developing countries demonstrates that many varieties of adaptation to defeat, or to the threat of it, are available to leaders of the liberation movement.

Notes

Chapter 1

1. For analysis of the intellectual and political trajectory of the ANC over the century of its existence, see A.M. Butler, *The Idea of the ANC* (Auckland Park, 2012).
2. F. Boucek, 'The maintenance and decline of dominant party systems in the developed world: Inter- and intra-party interpretations', Paper presented at a Dominant Party Systems Conference, University of Michigan, 9–10 May 2014, 1.
3. R.S. Katz and P. Mair, 'The cartel party thesis: A restatement', *Perspectives on Politics* 7, 4 (2009), 753–766.
4. R. Southall, *Liberation Movements in Power: Party and State in Southern Africa* (Scottsville, 2013).
5. Southall, *Liberation Movements in Power*, 3–5.
6. Southall, *Liberation Movements in Power*.
7. Southall, *Liberation Movements in Power*, 43.
8. Southall, *Liberation Movements in Power*, 139, 275, 43.
9. H. Giliomee and C.E.W. Simkins (eds), *The Awkward Embrace: One-party Domination and Democracy* (London, 1999).
10. E. Friedman and J. Wong (eds), *Political Transitions in Dominant Party Systems: Learning to Lose* (New York, 2008); M. Bogaards and F. Boucek (eds), *Dominant Political Parties and Democracy: Concepts, Measures, Cases and Comparisons* (New York, 2010); R. Doorenspleet and L. Nijzink (eds), *One-party Dominance in African Democracies* (Boulder, CO, 2013).
11. Friedman and Wong, *Political Transitions*, 9.
12. R. Harmel and K. Janda, 'The integrated theory of party change', *Journal of Theoretical Politics* 6, 3, (1994), 259–287.
13. K. Greene, *Why Dominant Parties Lose* (New York, 2007).
14. Martyn Davies, 'The ANC and the Chinese Communist Party', Presentation to a workshop on party reform, 17 January 2014, Cape Town. See also M. Davies, 'On my mind', *Financial Mail*, 2 April 2012.

Chapter 2

1. R.S. Katz and P. Mair, 'Changing models of party organization and party democracy: The emergence of the cartel party', *Party Politics* 1, 1 (1995), 5–28.

2   H. Chen, 'Party transformation toward "election machine" and the construction of its relationship with government: The experience of the KMT 2000–2102' (in Chinese), *Taiwanese Political Science Review* 17, 2 (2013), 15–70.
3   R. Harmel and K. Janda, 'The integrated theory of party change', *Journal of Theoretical Politics* 6, 3 (1994), 259–287.
4   A.C. Tan, 'The transformation of the Kuomintang Party in Taiwan', *Democratization* 9, 3 (2002), 149–164.
5   R. Harmel and A.C. Tan, 'Party actors and party change: Does factional dominance matter?', *European Journal of Political Research* 42, 3 (2003), 409–410.
6   K. Janda, 'Towards a performance theory of party change', Paper presented at the 12th World Congress of the International Sociological Association, Madrid, Spain, 1990, 5.
7   R. Harmel, K. Janda, U. Heo and A. Tan, 'Performance, leadership, factions and party change: An empirical analysis', *West European Politics* 18, 1 (1995), 1–33; T.N. Gilmore, *Making a Leadership Change: How Organizations and Leaders Can Handle Leadership Transitions Successfully* (London: Jossey-Bass, 1988); R. Michels, *Political Parties* (New York, 1962).
8   Gilmore, *Making a Leadership Change*, 11–14.
9   Michels, *Political Parties*.
10 Harmel et al., 'Performance, leadership, factions and party change'.
11 Harmel and Janda, 'The integrated theory of party change'.
12 Harmel and Tan, 'Party actors and party change'.
13 T. Cheng, 'Democratizing the quasi-Leninist regime in Taiwan', *World Politics* 41, 4 (1989), 471–499.
14 Chiang Ching-kuo concurrently held the position of party chairman and president of the Republic. In KMT's history in Taiwan since 1949, there were only two instances (1975–8 and 2008–9) wherein the president of the Republic is not the party chairman. Prior to Taiwan's transition to democracy in 1996, the concept of 'party-state' is a dominant paradigm in Taiwanese politics where the KMT (as the hegemonic and authoritarian party) dominates the state apparatus. The issue of separating or unifying the party chairmanship and the presidency (in times where the KMT holds the state presidency) became an important debating point in the KMT's reform in the democratic era.
15 Tan, 'The transformation of the Kuomintang Party in Taiwan'; Chen, 'Party transformation toward "election machine" and the construction of its relationship with government'.
16 C. Clark and A.C. Tan, *Taiwan's Political Economy: Meeting Challenges, Pursuing Progress* (Boulder, CO, 2012).
17 Prior to 1996, Taiwan's presidents were not popularly or directly elected by voters but elected by a National Assembly that is now defunct.
18 The 2004 presidential election was mired in controversy relating to a supposed assassination attempt on the last day of the election.
19 Janda, 'Towards a performance theory of party change'.
20 Tan, 'The transformation of the Kuomintang Party in Taiwan' has analysed KMT changes from 1988 to 2001.
21 Ibid., 160.
22 Chen, 'Party transformation toward "election machine" and the construction of its relationship with government'.
23 Tan, 'The transformation of the Kuomintang Party in Taiwan', 160.
24 Chen, 'Party transformation toward "election machine" and the construction of its relationship with government'.
25 Ibid.

26 Ibid.
27 D. Fell, 'Lessons of defeat: A comparison of Taiwanese ruling parties' responses to electoral defeat', *Asian Politics and Policy* 1, 4 (2009), 670.
28 Ibid.
29 Ibid.
30 H. Chen, 'The relative influence of the executive and the legislature on lawmaking' (in Chinese), *Humanities and Social Sciences Research* 5, 2 (2011), 77–103.
31 Chen, 'Party transformation toward "election machine" and the construction of its relationship with government'.
32 Ibid.
33 Clark and Tan, *Taiwan's Political Economy* discusses the institutional imbroglio and consequences of these institutions on Taiwan politics.
34 Chen, 'Party transformation toward "election machine" and the construction of its relationship with government'.
35 Harmel and Tan, 'Party actors and party change', 411.

Chapter 3

1 C. García, 'Vicente Fox: Todos podemos ser presidentes' (2010), http://mexico.cnn.com/nacional/2010/10/15/vicente-fox-los-lideres-del-mundo-y-los-nuevos-lideres, accessed 6 January 2014.
2 On the characteristics of dominant party regimes, see K.F. Greene, *Why Dominant Parties Lose: Mexico's Democratisation in Comparative Perspective* (Cambridge, 2007).
3 Ibid.
4 Ibid.
5 C. Aristegui, 'Manzur operaba con la anuencia de Javer Duarte' (audio recording 2013), http://aristeguinoticias.com/0605/mexico/audio-manzur-operaba-con-la-anuencia-de-javier-duarte, accessed 11 June 2014; E.L. Gibson, 'Boundary control: Subnational authoritarianism in democratic countries', *World Politics* 58, 1 (2005), 101–132; J. Gil Olmos, 'Las trampas electorales de Ulises Ruiz', *Proceso*, 6.21.2010.
6 L. Zuckermann, 'Los señores feudales van a querer garantías', *Nexos*, 8.1.2011.
7 A. Panebianco, *Political Parties: Organisation and Power* (Cambridge, 1988).
8 S.M. Lipset and S. Rokkan 'Cleavage structures, party systems, and voter alignments' in Lipset and Rokkan (eds), *Party Systems and Voter Alignments* (New York, 1967), 30; A. Przeworski and J. Sprague, *Paper Stones: A History of Electoral Socialism* (Chicago, 1986).
9 R. Michels, *Political Parties: A Sociological Study of the Oligarchical Tendencies of Modern Democracy* (Glencoe, 1949); S. Levitsky, *Transforming Labour-Based Parties in Latin America: Argentine Peronism in Comparative Perspective* (Cambridge, 2003).
10 R.B. Collier and D. Collier, *Shaping the Political Arena: Critical Junctures, the Labour Movement, and Regime Dynamics in Latin America* (Princeton, 1991).
11 A. Downs, *An Economic Theory of Democracy* (New York, 1967).
12 J.E. Roemer, *Political Competition* (Cambridge, MA, 2001).
13 F.P. Belloni and D.C. Beller, *Faction Politics: Political Parties and Factionalism in Comparative Perspective* (Santa Barbara, CA, 1978).
14 J.D. May, 'Opinion structure of political parties: The special law of curvilinear disparity', *Political Studies* 21, 2 (1976), 135–151.
15 D. Samuels 'From socialism to social democracy? The evolution of the Workers' Party in Brazil', *Comparative Political Studies* 37, 9 (2004), 999–1024; W. Hunter, *The Transformation of*

      the Workers' Party in Brazil, 1989–2009 (Cambridge, 2010).
16. Przeworski and Sprague, *Paper Stones*; H. Kitschelt, *The Transformation of European Social Democracy* (New York, 1994).
17. H. Aguilar Camín and L. Meyer, *In the Shadow of the Mexican Revolution: Contemporary Mexican History, 1910–1989* (Austin, TX, 1993).
18. B. Carr, *Marxism and Communism in Twentieth-Century Mexico* (Lincoln, NB, 1993).
19. Collier and Collier, *Shaping the Political Arena*.
20. L.J. Garrido, 'The crisis of presidencialismo' in W. Cornelius, J. Gentleman and P.H. Smith (eds), *Mexico's Alternative Political Futures* (La Jolla, CA, 1988).
21. B. Magaloni, 'Credible power-sharing and the longevity of authoritarian rule', *Comparative Political Studies* 41, 4–5 (2008), 726.
22. L.J. Garrido, *El Partido de la Revolución Institucionalizada* (Mexico City, 1982).
23. J. Molinar, *El Tiempo de la Legitimidad: Elecciones, Autoritarismo y Democracia en México* (Mexico City, 1991).
24. H. Ibarra-Rueda, 'Why factions matter: A theory of party dominance at the subnational level' (PhD thesis, University of Texas at Austin), 73–85.
25. Garrido, 'The crisis of presidencialismo'.
26. R.A. Camp, 'Mexican governors since Cárdenas: Education and career contacts', *Journal of Interamerican Studies and World Affairs* 16, 4 (1974), 456.
27. Ibarra, 'Why factions matter', 73–85. R. Hernández Rodríguez, *Amistades, Compromisos y Lealtades: Líderes y Grupos Políticos en el Estado de México, 1942–1993* (Mexico City, 1998).
28. R.H. Bates, A. Greif, M. Levi and J.L Rosenthal (eds), *Analytic Narratives* (Princeton, 1998).
29. J. Langston, *Democratization and Party Change: Mexico's Evolving PRI, 1980–2012* (Mexico City, 2014).
30. T.A. Eisenstadt, *Courting Democracy in Mexico: Party Strategies and Electoral Institutions* (Cambridge, 2004), 234–269.
31. R.D. Hansen, *The Politics of Mexican Development* (Baltimore, 1971).
32. N. Lustig, *Mexico: The Remaking of an Economy* (Washington, DC, 1988).
33. R. Duch and R. Stevenson, *The Economic Vote: How Political and Economic Institutions Condition Election Results* (New York, 2008).
34. J. Castañeda, *Perpetuating Power: How Mexican Presidents Were Chosen* (New York, 2000).
35. Langston, *Democratization and Party Change*.
36. T.A. Eisenstadt, 'Mexico's postelectoral concertaciones: The rise and demise of a substitutive informal institution' in G. Helmke and S. Levitsky (eds), *Informal Institutions and Democracy: Lessons from Latin America* (Baltimore, MD, 2006), 227–248.
37. F. Reveles Vázquez, *Partido Revolucionario Institucional: Crisis y Refundación* (Mexico City, 2003), 109–112; J. Langston, 'Why rules matter: Changes in candidate selection in Mexico's PRI, 1988–2000', *Journal of Latin American Studies* 33, 3 (2001), 498.
38. Greene, *Why Dominant Parties Lose*.
39. D. MacLeod, *Downsizing the State: Privatization and the Limits of Neo-Liberal Reform in Mexico* (University Park, PA, 2004).
40. T.P. Kessler, *Global Capital and National Politics: Reforming Mexico's Financial System* (Westport CT, 1999).
41. J. Molinar and J.A. Weldon, 'Electoral determinants and consequences of national solidarity', in W. Cornelius, A. Craig and J. Fox (eds), *Transforming State–Society Relations in Mexico: The National Solidarity Strategy* (La Jolla, CA, 1994).
42. A. Oppenheimer, *Bordering on Chaos: Guerrillas, Stockbroker, Politicians, and Mexico's Road to Prosperity* (Boston, 1996).

43 Greene, *Why Dominant Parties Lose*; A. Schedler, 'From electoral authoritarianism to democratic consolidation', in R. Crandall, G. Paz, and R. Riordan (eds), *Mexico's Democracy at Work: Political and Economic Dynamics* (Boulder, CO, 2005), 9–37.
44 Personal interview by Greene with Carlos Sobrino, director of the PRI's Territorial Movement organisation, 10 February 1999.
45 R. Hernández Rodríguez, 'Cambio político y renovación institucional: Las gubernaturas en México', *Foro Internacional* 43, 4 (2003), 789–821.
46 T. Kessler, 'The Mexican peso crash: Causes, consequences, comeback', in C. Wise and R. Roett (eds), *Exchange Rate Politics in Latin America* (Washington, DC, 2000).
47 Greene, *Why Dominant Parties Lose*, 102.
48 Greene, *Why Dominant Parties Lose*, 113.
49 Schedler, 'From electoral authoritarianism to democratic consolidation'.
50 Greene, *Why Dominant Parties Lose*.
51 Langston, *Democratization and Party Change*.
52 Gibson, 'Boundary control', 114–115.
53 A 2007 change to PRI statutes required half of all public funds to go to state party organisations (Langston, *Democratization and Party Change*, 156).
54 A. Diaz-Cayeros, 'Mexican federalism and the institutionalisation of the politics of governors', manuscript (La Jolla, CA, 2005).
55 Langston, *Democratization and Party Change*, 126.
56 C. Beer, 'Invigorating federalism: The emergence of governors and state legislatures as powerbrokers and policy innovators', in R.A. Camp (ed.), *The Oxford Handbook of Mexican Politics* (Oxford, 2012), 119–143.
57 V.E. Rodríguez, *Decentralization in Mexico: From Reforma Municipal to Solidaridad to Nuevo Federalismo* (Boulder, CO, 1997).
58 Langston, 'Why rules matter', 506–509.
59 Langston, *Democratization and Party Change*, 128–131.
60 Castañeda, *Perpetuating Power*.
61 J. Langston, 'Legislative recruitment in Mexico', in P.M. Siavelis and S. Morgenstern (eds), *Pathways to Power: Political Recruitment and Candidate Selection in Latin America* (University Park, PA, 2012), 156–157.
62 S.T. Wuhs, 'Democratization and the dynamics of candidate selection rule change in Mexico, 1991–2003', *Mexican Studies* 22, 1 (2006), 43.
63 Castañeda, *Perpetuating Power*.
64 Langston, *Democratization and Party Change*, chapter 3.
65 Camp, 'Mexican governors since Cárdenas'.
66 Ibarra, 'Why factions matter', 38–45.
67 Ibid., 54–57.
68 Greene, *Why Dominant Parties Lose*; K. Bruhn, *Taking on Goliath: The Emergence of a New Left Party and the Struggle for Democracy in Mexico* (University Park, PA, 1997).
69 Office of the President of Mexico, 'Pre-Election poll in Michoacán', 23 July 1995, http://hdl.handle.net/10089/3497, accessed 5 February 2011.
70 Ibarra, 'Why factions matter'.
71 Ibid., 68–74.
72 Office of the President of Mexico, 'Pre-Election poll in Zacatecas', 9 December 1997, http://hdl.handle.net/10089/3419, accessed 3 February 2011.
73 Ibarra, 'Why factions matter'.
74 K.F. Greene, 'The political economy of single-party dominance', *Comparative Political Studies*

43, 9 (2010), 1–27.
75 G. Gary, *Making Votes Count: Strategic Coordination in the World's Electoral Systems* (Cambridge, 1997); A. Hicken, *Building Party Systems in Developing Democracies* (Cambridge, 2009).

Chapter 4

1   For an account of UMNO's emergence as a dominant party, see D.A. Mauzy and S.J. Barter, 'Learning to lose? Not if UMNO can help it', in E. Friedman and J. Wong (eds), *Political Transitions in Dominant Party Systems: Learning to Lose* (London, 2008), 211–230.
2   E.T. Gomez, 'Monetizing politics: Financing parties and elections in Malaysia', *Modern Asian Studies* 46, 5 (2012), 1370–1397.
3   A. Zakaria, 'Malaysia: Quasi-democracy in a divided society', in L. Diamond, J.J. Linz and S.M. Lipset (eds.), *Democracy in Developing Countries, Volume Three: Asia* (Boulder, CO, 1989), 347–381; W. Case, 'Semi-democracy in Malaysia: Withstanding the pressures for regime change', *Pacific Affairs* 66, 2 (1993), 183–205; D. Slater and J. Wong, 'The strength to concede: Ruling parties and democratization in developmental Asia', *Perspectives on Politics* 11, 3 (2013), 717–731.
4   C. Johnson, *Miti and the Japanese Miracle: The Growth of Industrial Policy, 1925–1975* (Stanford, CA, 1982).
5   Ibid.; A. Amsden, *Asia's Next Giant: South Korea and Late Industrialisation* (New York, 1989); R. Wade, *Governing the Market: Economic Theory and the Role of Government in East Asian Industrialization* (Princeton, 1990).
6   D. Harvey, *A Brief History of Neoliberalism* (Oxford, 2005).
7   E.T. Gomez, 'The rise and fall of capital: Corporate Malaysia in historical perspective', *Journal of Contemporary Asia* 39, 3 (2009), 345–381.
8   The 13 May incident has been widely attributed to inter-ethnic economic inequities. New research, however, indicates that political elites precipitated this crisis because of UMNO's loss of electoral support during the 1969 election. See K.S. Kua, *May 13: Declassified Documents on the Malaysian Riots of 1969* (Kuala Lumpur, 2007).
9   J. Faaland, J.R. Parkinson and R.B. Saniman, *Growth and Ethnic Inequality: Malaysia's New Economic Policy* (Kuala Lumpur, 2003); E.T. Gomez and R. Premdas (eds), *Affirmative Action, Ethnicity and Conflict* (London, 2013).
10 In response to the riots, in the political arena, UMNO enlarged its tripartite alliance into a multi-party coalition, the BN, incorporating a number of opposition parties.
11 O. Mehmet, *Development in Malaysia: Poverty, Wealth and Trusteeship* (London, 1986).
12 For a study of the rise of well-connected Bumiputera businessmen, see P. Sloane, *Islam, Modernity and Entrepreneurship among the Malays* (Basingstoke, 1999).
13 For a critique of the implementation of privatisation, see K.S. Jomo (ed.), *Privatizing Malaysia: Rents, Rhetoric, Realities* (Boulder, CO, 1995); J. Tan, *Privatization in Malaysia: Regulation, Rent-seeking and Policy Failure* (London, 2008).
14 Jomo, *Privatizing Malaysia*.
15 Gomez, 'The rise and fall of capital'.
16 I.W. Hwang, *Personalized Politics: The Malaysian State under Mahathir* (Singapore, 2003).
17 See Mahathir's speech entitled 'The new Malay dilemma', delivered to the Harvard Club of Malaysia on 27 July 2002.
18 For details on the takeover of assets controlled by Anwar allies and Daim protégés, see *Far Eastern Economic Review*, 5 July 2001.
19 See the report entitled 'Overview of the 9th Malaysia Plan' by the Center for Public Policy

Studies at www.cpps.org.my.
20   Malaysia, *New Economic Model for Malaysia, Parts I & II* (Putrajaya, 2010).
21   Malaysia. *Tenth Malaysia Plan, 2011–2015* (Kuala Lumpur, 2010).
22   *Bernama*, 30 June 2009.
23   Sloane, *Islam, Modernity and Entrepreneurship among the Malays*.
24   R. Harmel, U. Heo, A. Tan and K. Janda, 'Performance, leadership, factions and party change: An empirical analysis', *West European Politics* 18, 1 (1995), 1–33.
25   E.T. Gomez (ed.), *The State of Malaysia: Ethnicity, Equity and Reform* (London, 2004).
26   W. Case, 'Malaysia: New reforms, old continuities, tense ambiguities', *Journal of Development Studies* 41, 2 (2005), 284–309.
27   Gomez and Premdas, *Affirmative Action, Ethnicity and Conflict*.
28   BN subsequently regained control of the state of Perak following defections from the opposition.
29   T.B. Pepinsky, *Economic Crises and the Breakdown of Authoritarian Regimes: Indonesia and Malaysia in Comparative Perspective* (Cambridge, 2009).
30   Slater and Wong, 'The strength to concede Asia'.

Chapter 5

1   G.S. Reis, 'Ainda a social-democracia?: Rediscutindo e aplicando o conceito a partidos competitivos da América do Sul e da Europa' (PhD thesis, IESP-UERJ, 2013).
2   The dominance of the pragmatist wing has increased as, according to Kitschelt's theory, new pragmatists and lobbyists enter the party attracted by the accessibility to office. Indeed, 77 per cent of PT members affiliated themselves to the party from 2001 (one year before Lula's victory) on, according to L. Secco, *História do PT* (Cotia, 2011), 249. For discussing lobbyists and pragmatists, see H. Kitschelt, 'Organization, strategy, and elections', in H. Kitschelt, *The Logics of Party Formation: Ecological Politics in Belgium and West Germany* (Ithaca and London, 1989), 41–74.
3   A. Singer, *O PT* (São Paulo, 2001); D. Samuels, 'From socialism to social democracy: Party organization and the transformation of the Workers' Party in Brazil', *Comparative Political Studies* 37, 9 (2004), 999–1024; Secco, *História do PT*. Singer says that until 1990 PT was still ambiguous in its view of democracy. Although the party had always supported free elections, Singer states that the party, divided into many factions, sometimes defended full democracy, understanding that the alternation of parties in government was part of the game; but sometimes it was not clear what PT would do after winning and achieving hegemony, if it would tolerate bourgeois parties and rivals of the working class. The Workers' Party's discourse was more radical in its origins and also in its first elections, but became moderated over time until 2002, when Lula presented himself in the election campaign as the moderate 'Lulinha love and peace' and had José Alencar, a businessman from the Liberal Party (PL), as his candidate for the vice-presidency.
4   See A. Przeworski, *Capitalism and Social Democracy* (Cambridge, 1985). That path can be systematised in four steps: firstly, the decision to take part in electoral and parliamentary democracy and to defend it; then, the understanding that reform is a better way than revolution and that elections are useful not only for propaganda; afterwards, the conclusion that it is necessary to build broader coalitions as the workers will not form a majority alone; finally, the social democratic party gives up socialism, supports gradual and cumulative improvements, and thereafter tries to manage capitalism.
5   Particularly in the region known as ABCD, which comprises the towns Santo André, São

Bernardo do Campo, São Caetano do Sul and Diadema. In that year, 328 strikes were held in that region between May and December, according to Secco, *História do PT*, 39.
6 Singer, *O PT*; Secco. *História do PT*; G.S. Reis and J. Medeiros, 'Partidos antineoliberais: As negligenciadas semelhanças entre o PT e o MAS', Paper presented at Annual Meeting of Anpocs, 2012.
7 PT, *Resoluções de Encontros e Congressos* (São Paulo, 1998), 56.
8 Ibid., 107.
9 I. Sarti, *Da Outra Margem do Rio: Os Partidos Políticos em Busca da Utopia* (Rio de Janeiro, 2006), 26; Secco, *História do PT*, 118–119.
10 Secco, *História do PT*, 47–49. According to Secco (51), the far left has been important within the PT only in regions where the party's social basis was weak.
11 PT took part in these elections in 23 of the 25 Brazilian states, but elected only eight federal deputies, six of them from São Paulo state. In all the country, 3 941 seats in local level assemblies were contested, but PT obtained only 117. In the elections for state governor, the only candidate from the Workers' Party with significant votes was Lula, who ran in São Paulo and got ten per cent of the votes. PT elected only two mayors, one of them in Diadema, in the ABCD region, and the other in the tiny town of Santa Quitéria, in the north-eastern state of Maranhão, but the latter moved to another party soon after being elected. See Singer, *O PT*.
12 Other members also participated in the building of Articulation, such as many leftists from Catholic Church, most of the intellectuals from São Paulo and many from PCB or PC do B who had participated in armed struggle. See Secco, *História do PT*; Reis and Medeiros. 'Partidos antineoliberais'.
13 Sarti, *Da Outra Margem do Rio*, 24–25.
14 Secco, *História do PT*, 77–92.
15 Ibid., 94–7 and 123; Reis and Medeiros, 'Partidos antineoliberais'.
16 Singer, *O PT*; Secco. *História do PT*.
17 Reis and Medeiros, 'Partidos antineoliberais'.
18 Sarti, *Da Outra Margem do Rio*, 25.
19 Reis and Medeiros, 'Partidos antineoliberais'.
20 Ibid., 75.
21 Ibid., 185–186.
22 P.J.F. Ribeiro, 'Dos sindicatos ao governo: A organização nacional do PT de 1980 a 2005' (PhD thesis, Universidade Federal de São Carlos, 2008).
23 R. Katz and P. Mair, 'Changing models of party organization and party democracy: The emergence of the cartel party', *Party Politics* 1, 1 (1995).
24 D. Samuels, 'O financiamento de campanhas no Brasil e propostas de reforma', in G.A.D. Soares and L. Rennó (eds), *Reforma Política: Lições da História Recente* (Rio de Janeiro, 2006). Lula's presidential campaign received R$3.5 million in 1998 and 26.5 million in 2002.
25 Secco, *História do PT*, 194–195.
26 That is what the Movement Towards Socialism (MAS) has done in Bolivia, by attaching the vote for the president to the vote for the senator and for party lists in the lower chamber, benefiting from the large voting of Evo Morales. See C. Zucco, 'O legislativo no conflito político Boliviano', *Papéis Legislativos* 3, 1 (2009); C. Cunha Filho, 'O Novo mapa político Boliviano: Uma interpretação a partir dos ultimos resultados eleitorais', *Observador On-line* 5, 6 (2010). Indeed, PT would probably be assisted by the adoption of closed lists, which the party has always supported, and by correcting malapportionment.
27 A. Singer, *Os sentidos do Lulismo: Reforma Gradual e Pacto Conservador* (São Paulo, 2012).

Chapter 6

1. *People's Daily*, 'Zhongguo wangmin shuliang da 6.04 yi (China's Internet users reached 604 millions)', 29 November 2013, http://media.people.com.cn/n/2013/1129/c40606-23691311.html, accessed 1 December 2013.
2. Basic data, China Internet Network Information Center, www1.cnnic.cn/IDR/BasicData/, accessed 19 July 2013.
3. Xinhua Net,'Sina Weibo user numbers surpassed 500 million', 21 March 2013, www.cq.xinhuanet.com/2013-02/21/c_114749460.htm, accessed 5 July 2013.
4. Yin Yungong, *Zhongguo xin meiti fazhan nianbao (Annual Report on the Development of New Media in China)* (Beijing, 2011).
5. Dou Hanzhang and Li Moning (eds), *Zhengfu Ruhe Kai Weibo (How Should the Government Set up a Weibo Account)* (Beijing, 2011), 3.
6. People's Daily Online, 'Zhu Xinhua: Wangluo yulun daobi zhongguo gaige (Zhu Xinhua: Internet public opinion pushed forward China's reform)', 9 October 2011, www.21ccom.net/articles/zgyj/gqmq/2011/1014/46984.html, accessed 18 July 2013.
7. China Net, 'Shibada hou 11 wei shengbuji guanyuan luoma (11 officials at the provincial level were sent down since the 18th National Congress for the CCP)', 14 November 2013, http://legal.china.com.cn/2013-11/14/content_30597269_2.htm, accessed 1 December 2013.
8. Opinion on the role of social media in Iran's 2009 protest and the Arab Spring remains divided among scholars. Some argue that conversations about revolution often preceded major events on the ground, and social media carried inspiring stories of protest across international borders.
9. BBC Chinese, 'Zhao Qizheng: "Jasmine Revolution" will not take place in China', 24 February 2011, www.bbc.co.uk/zhongwen/trad/china/2011/02/110224_jasmine_protest_patience.shtml, accessed 7 July 2013.
10. Tai Zixue, *The Internet in China: Cyberspace and Civil Society* (London, 2006).
11. Yang Guobin, *The Power of the Internet in China: Citizen Activism Online* (New York, 2009), 3, 44.
12. Zheng Yongnian, *Technological Empowerment: The Internet, State, and Society in China* (Stanford, CA, 2007).
13. Jens Damm, 'The Internet and the Fragmentation of Chinese Society', *Critical Asian Studies* 39, 2 (2007), 273–294.
14. David Shambaugh, *China's Communist Party: Atrophy and Adaptation* (Berkeley, CA, 2008); Michael Chase and James Mulvenon, *You've Got Dissent: Chinese Dissident Use of the Internet and Beijing's Counter-Strategies* (2002), xiii.
15. Zhou Yongming, *Historicizing Online Politics: Telegraphy, the Internet, and Political Participation in China* (Stanford, CA, 2006).
16. Andrew J. Nathan, 'Authoritarian resilience', *Journal of Democracy* 14, 1 (2003), 6–17.
17. Zheng Yongnian, *The Chinese Communist Party as Organizational Emperor: Culture, Reproduction, and Transformation* (London, 2010).
18. Xinhua Net, 'Hu Jintao zai xuanchuan huiyi jianghua: yong sange daibiao tongling xuanchuan gongzuo (Hu Jingtao's speech at the propaganda work conference: Command propaganda works with three representations)', 7 December 2003, http://news.xinhuanet.com/newscenter/2003-12/07/content_1218040.htm, accessed 12 July 2013.
19. Xinhua Net, 'Guanyu jiaqiang dang zhizheng nengli jianshe de jueding (Decision of the CCP Central Committee on strengthening the party's ruling ability)', 26 September 2004, http://news.xinhuanet.com/newscenter/2004-09/26/content_2024232.htm, accessed 12

July 2013.
20 Ibid.
21 General Administration of Press and Publication, 'Xinwen chuban zongshu caiqu cuoshi, jiaqiang wangluo wenhua jianshe he guanli (The General Administration of Press and Publication takes measure to strengthen the construction and regulation of online culture)', www.wangbianzheng.com/NewsView-94.aspx, accessed 12 June 2013.
22 Xinhua Net, 'Hu Jintao: yi chuangxin jingshen jiaqiang wangluo wenhua jianshe guanli (Hu Jintao: strengthening the construction and regulation of online culture with innovative spirit).' 24 January 2007, http://news.xinhuanet.com/politics/2007-01/24/content_5648188.htm, accessed 10 June 2013.
23 Ibid.
24 General Administration of Press and Publication, 'Xinwen chuban zongshu caiqu cuoshi, jiaqiang wangluo wenhua jianshe he guanli (The General Administration of Press and Publication takes measure to strengthen the construction and regulation of online culture)'.
25 China News Agency, 'Zhongyang tichu jiaqiang wangluo wenhua guanli (The Central Committee advocates the strengthening of Internet culture management)', 25 October 2011, www.chinanews.com/gn/2011/10-25/3414069.shtml, accessed 10 June 2013.
26 Zheng Yongnian, *The Chinese Communist Party as Organizational Emperor*, 14–15.
27 Government Online Project Service Center, 'Zoujin xin shidai (Entering a new era)', quoted in Zhang Junhua, 'Will the government "serve the people": The development of Chinese e-government', *New Media and Society* 4, 2 (2002), 163–184.
28 Ibid.
29 Improvement and Development Agency, 'Local e-government now: A worldwide view' (2002), www.sap.com/solutions/industry/publicsector, accessed 30 June 2013.
30 Zhou Xiang, 'E-government in China: A content analysis of national and provincial web sites', *Journal of Computer-Mediated Communication* 9 (2004), doi: 10.1111/j.1083-6101.2004.tb00297.x, accessed 16 May 2013.
31 *People's Daily*, 'Luo Hua: 51 wei shengweishuji shengzhang zai renminwang difang lingdao liuyanban duihua wangmin (Luo Hua: 51 party chiefs and governors interact with netizens via leaders message boards)', 28 November 2013, http://politics.people.com.cn/n/2013/1128/c1001-23683337.html, accessed 1 December 2013.
32 People's Daily Online, http://leaders.people.com.cn/, accessed 15 May 2013.
33 *People's Daily*, 'Renminwang difang lingdao liuyanban si sui le (Four year anniversary of People's Daily Online local leaders message board)' (2010), http://leaders.people.com.cn/GB/70158/200464/, accessed 1 December 2013.
34 *People's Daily*, 'Luo Hua: 51 wei shengweishuji shengzhang zai renminwang difang lingdao liuyanban duihua wangmin (Luo Hua: 51 party chiefs and governors interact with netizens via leaders message boards)'.
35 Ibid.
36 *People's Daily*, 'Renminwang difang lingdao liuyanban si sui le (Four year anniversary of People's Daily Online local leaders message board)'.
37 *People's Daily*, 'Luo Hua: 51 wei shengweishuji shengzhang zai renminwang difang lingdao liuyanban duihua wangmin (Luo Hua: 51 party chiefs and governors interact with netizens via leaders message boards)'.
38 People's Daily Public Opinion Monitoring Office, 'Annual report of government account on Sina Weibo 2012', December 2012, http://yuqing.people.com.cn/NMediaFile/2012/1203/MAIN201212031436000123338318108.pdf, accessed 7 June 2013.
39 Ministry of Public Security, 'Gonganbu zai Beijing juxing Weibo huiyi (Minister of Public

Security held police Weibo conference in Beijing)', 26 September 2011, www.gov.cn/gzdt/2011-09/26/content_1957013.htm, accessed 14 June 2013.
40 Xinhua Net, 'Zhengfu Weibo youxue yourou cai neng hold zhu minxin (Government Weibo has to uphold a down-to-earth manner)', 21 March 2012, http://news.xinhuanet.com/politics/2012-03/21/c_122858641_2.htm, accessed 12 June 2013.
41 People's Daily Public Opinion Monitoring Office, 'Annual report of government account on Sina Weibo 2012'.
42 Chris Buckley, 'Crackdown on bloggers is mounted by China,' 10 September 2013, www.nytimes.com/2013/09/11/world/asia/china-cracks-down-on-online-opinion-makers.html?pagewanted=1&_r=0, accessed 29 November 2013.
43 *The Economist*, 'Big Vs and bottom lines', 31 August 2013, www.economist.com/news/china/21584385-authorities-move-against-some-chinas-most-vocal-microbloggers-big-vs-and-bottom-lines, accessed 29 November 2013.
44 Chris Buckley, 'Crackdown on bloggers is mounted by China'.
45 Megha Rajagopalan, 'China's rumour crackdown has "cleaned" Internet, official says', 28 November 2013, http://in.reuters.com/article/2013/11/28/china-Internet-idINDEE9AR08K20131128, accessed 29 November 2013.
46 Xinhua News, 'Zhongjiwei wangzhan kaitong (CCDI website launched)', 26 September 2013, http://news.xinhuanet.com/politics/2013-09/26/c_125447841.htm, accessed 30 November 2013.
47 Xinhua News, 'Party discipline agency vows timely exposure of corruption', 12 September 2013, http://news.xinhuanet.com/english/china/2013-09/12/c_132715811.htm, accessed 30 November 2013.
48 CCDI and Ministry of Supervision, www.ccdi.gov.cn/, accessed 29 November 2013.
49 CCDI and Ministry of Supervision Report, www.12388.gov.cn/, accessed 30 November 2013.
50 Xinhua News, 'Zhongjiwei wangzhan kaitong (CCDI website launched)'.
51 Ibid.
52 Zheng Yongnian, *The Chinese Communist Party as Organizational Emperor*, 39.
53 Wang Zhengxu, 'Political trust in China: Forms and causes' in Lynn White (ed.), *Legitimacy: Ambiguities of Political Success or Failure in East and Southeast Asia* (Singapore, 2005).
54 Yu Jianrong, 'An investigation of the petitioning system and thoughts on its reform', in *2005 China Social Situation Analysis and Forecast* (Beijing, 2005).
55 Sina Weibo, 'Report on government Weibo on Sina' (2013), http://vdisk.Weibo.com, accessed 20 May 2013.
56 Jiang Min, 'Authoritarian deliberation on Chinese internet', *Electronic Journal of Communication* 20, 3/4 (2010).
57 *China Daily*, 'Jiangxi officials sacked after protesters burn themselves', 20 September 2010, www.chinadaily.com.cn/china/2010-09/20/content_11325621.htm, accessed 2 December 2013.
58 John C. Bertot, Paul T. Jaeger and Justin M. Grimes, 'Using ICTs to create a culture of transparency: E-government and social media as openness and anti-corruption tools for societies', *Government Information Quarterly* 27, 3 (2010), 264–271.
59 United Nations and American Society for Public Administration, *Benchmarking E-government: A Global Perspective* (New York, 2002), 1.
60 James S.L. Yong (ed.), *E-government in Asia: Enabling Public Service Innovation in the 21st Century* (Singapore, 2005).
61 Shanthi Kalathil and Taylor Boas, 'The internet and state control in authoritarian regimes:

China, Cuba, and the counterrevolution', *Global Policy Program* 21 (July 2001), www.ceip.org/files/pdf/21KalathilBoas.pdf, accessed 11 April 2013.
62 Ma Lianjie, Jongpil Chung and Stuart Thorson, 'E-government in China: Bringing economic development through administrative reform', *Government Information Quarterly* 22, 1 (2005), 20–37.
63 State Council, Regulations of the People's Republic of China on Open Government Information (2007), www.gov.cn/zwgk/2007-04/24/content_592937.htm, accessed 30 April 2013.
64 Valentine Ndou, 'E-government for developing countries: Opportunities and challenges', *Electronic Journal of Information Systems in Developing Countries* 18 (2004).
65 The number of countries or territories included in the index also expended significantly, from 52 in 1997 to 177 in 2012. For CPI in each year, visit www.transparency.org/, accessed 29 November 2013.
66 Zhengyi Wang, 23 May 2013, http://zjby.jcrb.com/tzgg/201306/t20130630_1146257.shtml, accessed 29 November 2013.
67 CCP News, 'He Guoqian zai shiqi jie zhongjiwei di wu ci quanti huiyi shang de jianghua (quanwen) (He Guoqian's speech on the Fifth Plenum of 17th CCP CCDI)', 10 February 2010, http://cpc.people.com.cn/GB/64093/64094/10961809.html, accessed 29 November 2013.
68 Xinhua News, 'Woguo wangluo fanfu cheng gongmin canzheng zhongyao xingshi (Our country's Internet anti-corruption becomes an important means of civil participation)', 6 January 2011, http://news.xinhuanet.com/politics/2011-01/06/c_12953016.htm, accessed 2 December 2013.
69 Zheng Yongnian, *The Chinese Communist Party as Organizational Emperor*, 140.

Chapter 7
1 S. Nagi, 'Congress rout: A Sonia-Rahul guide on how to lose an election', *Firstpost*, 2014.
2 F. Boucek, 'Rethinking factionalism: Typologies, intra-party dynamics and three faces of factionalism', *Party Politics* 15 (2009), 469.
3 S. Biswas, 'Was India's PM Manmohan Singh undermined by own party?', *BBC News*, www.bbc.com/news/world-asia-india-27018899, accessed 1 July 2014; Singabakho Nxumalo, 'Two centres of power', *News24*, www.news24.com/MyNews24/YourStory/Two-centres-of-power-20070704, accessed 1 July 2014.
4 Boucek, 'Rethinking factionalism', 469.
5 Ibid.
6 Ibid., 473.
7 Ibid., 476.
8 Q. Mtyala, 'Zuma's monster cabinet to cost SA R1bn', www.timeslive.co.za/thetimes/2014/05/28/zuma-s-monster-cabinet-to-cost-sa-r1bn, accessed 27 June 2014.
9 R.L. Hardgrave, 'The Congress in India: Crisis and split', *Asian Survey* 10 (1970), 256–262.
10 R.W. Johnson, 'False start in South Africa', *New Left Review* 58 (2009), 61–74.
11 M. Prasad Singh, 'The crisis of the Indian state: From quiet developmentalism to noisy democracy', *Asian Survey* 30 (1990), 815.
12 R. Suttner, 'Transformation of political parties in Africa today', *Transformation* 2004, 1–27.
13 S. Kaviraj, 'On state, society and discourse in India', in J. Manor (ed.), *Rethinking Third World Politics* (London, 1991), 72–99.
14 R. Joshi and R.K. Hebsur, *Congress in Indian politics* (London, 1987).

15   Ibid., 5.
16   S.A. Kochanek, *The Congress Party of India: The dynamics of one-party democracy* (Princeton, NJ, 1968).
17   Ibid., 135–150.
18   R. Kothari, 'The Congress system in India', *Asian Survey* 4 (1964), 1161–1173.
19   M. Weiner, *Party Building in a New Nation* (Chicago, 1967).
20   Ibid., 14.
21   Kothari, 'The Congress system in India'; W.H. Morris-Jones, 'Dominance and dissent: Their inter-relations in the Indian party system', *Government and Opposition* 1 (1966), 451–466.
22   Kothari, 'The Congress system in India'; R. Kothari, *Politics in India* (London, 1970); Morris-Jones, 'Dominance and dissent'.
23   Morris-Jones, 'Dominance and dissent', 217.
24   A.K. Lal, 'Dynamics of village factionalism: A case study of conflict between traditional and emerging leadership', *Journal of Social and Economic Studies* 1 (1973), 217–231.
25   S. Kaviraj, 'The post-colonial state: The special case of India', *Critical Encounters*, 2009, http://criticalencounters.net/2009/01/19/the-post-colonial-state-sudipta-kaviraj/.
26   S. Ghose, *Jawaharlal Nehru: A biography* (New Delhi, 1993), 175.
27   Kochanek, *The Congress Party of India*, 59.
28   S. Kaviraj, *Politics in India*, Oxford in India Readings in Sociology and Social Anthropology (Delhi, Oxford University Press, 1997).
29   Ibid., 21.
30   S. Kaviraj and S. Khilnani (eds), *Civil Society: History and Possibilities* (Cambridge, 2001), 21.
31   R. Suttner, 'The Zuma era: Its historical context and the future', *African Historical Review* 41 (2009), 28–59.
32   Hardgrave, 'The Congress in India', 257.
33   Ibid.
34   Singh, 'The crisis of the Indian state', 811.
35   G. Gerhart, *Black Power in South Africa: The Evolution of an Ideology* (Berkeley, CA, 1978).
36   Steven Friedman and Doreen Atkinson (eds), *The Small Miracle: South Africa's Negotiated Settlement* (Randburg: Ravan Press, 1994).
37   A. Odendaal, *Vukani Bantu! The Beginnings of Black Protest Politics in South Africa to 1912* (Cape Town, 1984).
38   Suttner, 'The Zuma era'.
39   H. Adam, 'The Mandela personality cult', *Indicator South Africa* 13 (1996).
40   A. Feinstein, *After the Party* (Johannesburg, 2007).
41   S.J. Terreblanche, *A History of Inequality in South Africa, 1652–2002* (Pietermaritzburg, 2002).
42   H. Marais, *South Africa: The Limits to Change* (London, 1998); J. Heintz, 'Gear: A labour perspective', *Indicator South Africa* 14 (1997), 252–261; Terreblanche, *A History of Inequality in South Africa*.

Chapter 8

1   Mail&Guardian Online, 7.12.2012, http://mg.co.za/article/2012-07-12-anc-cadre-deployment.
2   Notable examples include P. Kopecký, 'Political competition and party patronage: Public appointments in Ghana and South Africa', *Political Studies* 59 (2011), 713–732; K.J. Maphunye, 'Re-politicizing the bureaucracy to solve apartheid's inequalities? The political-administrative interface in South Africa', *Journal of Public Administration* 40, 3.1 (2005), 212–228; R. Cameron,

'Patronage in South African local government' (unpublished manuscript, 2011).
3 See S. Booysen, *The African National Congress and the Regeneration of Political Power* (Johannesburg, 2011) for a timeline on deployment; F. Potgieter-Gqubule, 'The institutional evolution of the ANC as party of government after 1994', in D. Plaatjies (ed.), *Future Inheritance: Building State Capacity in Democratic South Africa* (Johannesburg, 2011).
4 African National Congress, 'National Consultative Conference, National Preparatory Committee Documents', 1985, www.anc.org.za/show.php?id=134, accessed 19 February 2014.
5 African National Congress, '50th National Conference Resolutions: Building the ANC', 1997, www.anc.org.za/show.php?id=2427.
6 Ibid.
7 Ibid.
8 D. Posel, 'Labour relations and the politics of patronage: A case study of the apartheid civil service', in G. Adler (ed.), *Public Service Labour Relations in a Democratic South Africa* (Johannesburg, 2000).
9 V.T. Maphai, 'The civil service: Transition and affirmative action' in P. Hugo (ed.), *Redistribution and Affirmative Action: Working on the South African Political Economy* (Johannesburg, 1992).
10 H. Giliomee, J. Myburgh and L. Schlemmer, 'Dominant party rule, opposition parties and minorities in South Africa', *Democratization* 8, 1 (2001), 169.
11 Department of Public Service and Administration, White Paper on Affirmative Action in the Public Service (Pretoria, 1998).
12 Department of Public Service and Administration, White Paper on Human Resource Management in the Public Service (Pretoria, 1997).
13 Republic of South Africa, *Report of the Presidential Review Commission on the Reform and Transformation of the Public Service in South Africa* (1998), www.info.gov.za/otherdocs/1998/prc98/index.html.
14 Kopecký, 'Political competition and party patronage', 726.
15 H.M. Maserumule, 'Conflicts between directors-general and ministers in South Africa: 1994–2004: A "postulative" approach', *Politikon* 34, 2 (2007), 155, 160.
16 R. Cameron, 'Redefining political-administrative relationships in South Africa', *International Review of Administrative Sciences* 76, 4 (2010), 686, 687, 698.
17 The author did not identify departments by name.
18 Maphunye, 'Re-politicizing the bureaucracy', 223.
19 Public Service Commission, 'The turn-over rate of heads of department and its implications for the Public Service' (Pretoria, 2008).
20 Department of Public Service and Administration, 'Improving the performance of the public service: Lessons of the transformation process' (Pretoria, 2007).
21 Based on a 49 per cent response rate.
22 Public Service Commission, 'The turn-over rate of heads of department', x, 9.
23 Ibid., 20.
24 Public Service Commission, 'Fact sheet on the turnover rate of heads of department pre- and post-2009 general elections' (Pretoria, 2010), 1.
25 R. Cameron, 'Patronage in South African local government'.
26 Kopecký, 'Political competition and party patronage', 727.
27 Republic of South Africa, Local Government: Municipal Systems Amendment Act, 2011 (Cape Town, 2011).
28 N. de Jager, 'No "new" ANC?', *Politikon* 36, 2 (2009), 283, 285.

29   Giliomee, Myburgh, and Schlemmer, 'Dominant party rule', 173.
30   D. Plaatjies, 'Values, political governance and deployment' in Plaatjies, *Future Inheritance*, 100.
31   W. Gumede, 'South African state-owned enterprises: Boards, executives and recruitment: South African Presidential Review Committee on State-Owned Enterprises (PRC)' (2012), 50.
32   S. Seepe, 'A strategic agenda for organisational renewal: Much ado about nothing', in O. Edigheji (ed.), *Re-thinking South Africa's Development Path: Reflections on the ANC's Policy Conference Discussion Documents* (Johannesburg, 2007), 51.
33   There is an interesting parallel between Seepe's description of the ANC and Kopecký and Scherlis's description of changing forms of patronage in European party–state relations, in which societal links and a mass-based and activist character have given way to the benefits that control over state institutions brings, in terms of policy and organisational survival.
34   Cited in T. Lodge, 'The ANC and the development of party politics in modern South Africa', *Journal of Modern African Studies* 42, 2 (2004), 216.
35   Cited in Potgieter-Gqubule, 'The institutional evolution of the ANC as party of government after 1994', 89.
36   Booysen, *The African National Congress*.
37   African National Congress, '51st National Conference: Report of the Secretary General' (2002), www.anc.org.za/show.php?id=2494.
38   African National Congress, '51st National Conference: Resolutions' (2002), www.anc.org.za/show.php?id=2495.
39   African National Congress, '52nd National Conference: Resolutions' (2007), www.anc.org.za/show.php?id=2536.
40   F. Chikane, *Eight days in September: The removal of Thabo Mbeki* (Johannesburg, 2012), 105–106.
41   African National Congress, '53rd National Conference: Resolutions' (2012), www.anc.org.za/docs/res/2013/resolutions53r.pdf.
42   See for example H-U. Derlien, 'The politicization of bureaucracies in historical and comparative perspective', in B.G. Peters and B.A. Rockman (eds), *Agenda for Excellence 2: Administering the State* (Chatham, NJ, 1996); B.G. Peters and J. Pierre, 'Politicization of the civil service: Concepts, causes, consequences', in B.G. Peters and J. Pierre (eds), *Politicization of the Civil Service in Comparative Perspective* (London, 2004); and L. Rouban, 'Politicization of the civil service', in B.G. Peters and J. Pierre (eds), *Handbook of Public Administration* (Thousand Oaks, CA, 2003).
43   Peters and Pierre, 'Politicization of the civil service', 2.
44   An OECD study which assessed the level of political involvement in the staffing of senior bureaucrats found that in the South African case, directors-general and their deputies were considered 'political', while chief director and director appointments were described as 'hybrid', where administrative criteria was combined with 'political considerations'. A. Matheson et al., 'Study on the political involvement in senior staffing and on the delineation of responsibilities between ministers and senior civil servants', OECD Working Papers on Public Governance (Paris, 2007), 15.
45   V. Naidoo, 'Cadre deployment versus merit? Reviewing politicisation in the public service', in J. Daniel et al. (eds), *New South African Review 3: The Second Phase – Tragedy or Farce?* (Johannesburg, 2013).
46   Kopecký, 'Political competition and party patronage', 724.
47   National Planning Commission, *Our Future: Make it Work*, National Development Plan 2030 (Pretoria, 2012), 412, 414.
48   Kopecký, 'Political competition and party patronage', 717; P. Kopecký and G. Scherlis, 'Party

patronage in contemporary Europe', *European Review* 16, 3 (2008), 356.
49 McCourt refers to patronage as 'monelyess corruption'. W. McCourt, 'Public appointments: From patronage to merit', Human Resources in Development Group Working Paper Series, Working Paper No. 9 (Manchester, n.d.), 2.
50 Kopecký, 'Political competition and party patronage', 717.
51 Ibid., 727. Kopecký includes under the banner of 'control' attempts by parties to fulfil policy commitments through the state machinery.
52 Ibid., 726.
53 Booysen, *The African National Congress*, 383–384.
54 ANC, '51st National Conference: Report of the Secretary General'.
55 R. Southall, 'The "dominant party debate" in South Africa', *Afrika Spectrum* 39, 1 (2005), 64, 66.
56 Southall, 'The "dominant party debate"', 75.
57 African National Congress, '53rd National Conference: Resolutions'.
58 The importance of policy doctrine is captured in Rothstein's intriguing description of the 'cadre organisation' drawn from observations of the state–party relationship in the Peoples Republic of China. B. Rothstein, 'Understanding the quality of government in China: The cadre administration hypothesis', QoG Working Paper Series, 17 (Gothenburg, 2012).

Chapter 9

1 The paper largely draws on Chapters 1–7 and Chapter 11 of the 2012 document, as well as the section of Chapter 8 relating to grassroots development activism and participatory democracy.
2 Prior to 2012, the documents which in some way comprised a review or assessment of the movement since 1994 include: African National Congress, 'Organisational Democracy and Discipline in the Movement', 50th National Conference discussion document (1 July 1997), www.anc.org.za/show.php?id=308; African National Congress, 'The Character of the ANC', 50th National Conference discussion document (1 July 1997), www.anc.org.za/show.php?id=2026ANC; African National Congress, 'ANC: People's Movement and Agent for Change', ANC National General Council (NGC), (1 July 2000), www.anc.org.za/show.php?id=2358; and African National Congress, 'Towards the Centenary of the ANC: Discussion Document on Organisational Review: A Strategic Agenda for Organisational Renewal' (30 March 2007), www.anc.org.za/show.php?id=2365.
3 See ANC, 'People's Movement and Agent for Change' (1 July 2000) and ANC, 'Towards the Centenary of the ANC' (30 March 2007).
4 African National Congress, 'Organisational Renewal: Building the ANC as a Movement for Transformation and a Strategic Centre of Power', Discussion Document towards the National Policy Conference (10 April 2012), www.anc.org.za/docs/discus/2012/organisationalrenewalf.pdf, 5.
5 African National Congress, '52nd National Conference: Resolutions' (20 December 2007), www.anc.org.za/show.php?id=2536.
6 Congress of South African Trade Unions, 'Organisational Renewal: Building the ANC as a Movement for Transformation and a Strategic Centre of Power: Cosatu's Response' (2012), www.cosatu.org.za/docs/discussion/2012/organisational.pdf, 1–2.
7 African National Congress, 'Report of the Commission on Organisational Renewal', ANC National Policy Conference (30 June 2007), www.anc.org.za/show.php?id=2380.
8 ANC, 'Towards the Centenary of the ANC' (30 March 2007).

9   ANC, 'Organisational Renewal' (10 April 2012), 20.
10 Ibid., 63.
11 Ibid., 24.
12 African National Congress, '53rd National Conference: Resolutions' (31 Jan 2013), www.anc.org.za/list.php?t=Resolutions&y=2013, 8.
13 ANC, 'Organisational Renewal' (10 April 2012), 4.
14 Ibid., 4.
15 Ibid., 66.
16 Ibid., 5.
17 Ibid., 12.
18 Cosatu, 'Organisational Renewal' (2012), 4.
19 R. Southall, *Liberation Movements in Power: Party and State in Southern Africa* (Pietermaritzburg, 2013), 293.
20 ANC, 'Organisational Renewal' (10 April 2012), 4.
21 Ibid., 6–7, 9.
22 African National Congress, 'State of Organisation: From Resistance to Reconstruction and Nation-Building', 49th National Conference of the ANC, Bloemfontein (17–21 December 1994), www.anc.org.za/show.php?id=2410, accessed 19 November 2013.
23 The 2012 National Policy Conference of the ANC originally posited the idea of the 'second transition' which sought not only to mark its centenary conference as a watershed but also proposed the need for a new social and economic development path unlike that which had characterised the first two decades of democracy. However, disagreement within the ANC leadership as to how the 'second transition' marked a departure from the first led instead to its replacement by 'the second phase of transition' (Southall, *Liberation Movements in Power*, 321–2).
24 In 2008 in a speech to business, President Zuma referred to a position of 'continuity in change' in reference to continuing with practices that had been successful, but changing those that had not worked well. See S. Booysen, *The African National Congress and the Regeneration of Political Power* (Johannesburg, 2011), 93.
25 ANC, 'Organisational Renewal' (10 April 2012), 9–10.
26 Ibid., 5.
27 Ibid., 3.
28 ANC, 'Adopted Strategy and Tactics of the ANC: Building a National Democratic Society', 52nd National Conference of the ANC (20 December 2007), www.anc.org.za; ANC, '53rd National Conference: Resolutions' (31 January 2013), 8–9.
29 Booysen, *The African National Congress*, 113.
30 Southall, *Liberation Movements in Power*, 188.
31 ANC, 'Organisational Renewal' (10 April 2012), 11–12.
32 Ibid., 12.
33 ANC, 'Organisational Renewal' (10 April 2012), 57–58.
34 Ibid., 58.
35 Ibid. 58–59. See also ANC, '53rd National Conference: Resolutions' (31 January 2013), 8.
36 ANC, 'Organisational Renewal' (10 April 2012), 58.
37 Ibid., 12. See also 17–18.
38 Cosatu, 'Organisational Renewal' (2012), 16.
39 ANC, 'Organisational Renewal' (10 April 2012), 58.
40 Ibid., 16.
41 Ibid., 18.

42 Ibid.
43 Ibid., 17.
44 Ibid.
45 Ibid., 17.
46 Cosatu, 'Organisational Renewal' (2012), 6–7.
47 ANC, 'Organisational Renewal' (10 April 2012), 41.
48 Ibid., 23.
49 African National Congress, 'Conference Decisions and Recommendations from Commission Report on Strategy and Tactics', Consultative Conference of the ANC, Kabwe, Zambia (1985), Mayibuye Centre, ANC Lusaka Collection (MCH01), Box 47, Folder 47.3.
50 ANC, 'Organisational Renewal' (10 April 2012), 14.
51 Ibid., 18.
52 ANC, '50th National Conference: Resolutions – Building the ANC' (22 December 1997), www.anc.org.za/show.php?id=2427; ANC, '51st National Conference: Resolutions' (20 December 2002), www.anc.org.za/show.php?id=2495; ANC, '52nd National Conference: Resolutions' (20 December 2007), www.anc.org.za/show.php?id=2536.
53 ANC, 'Towards the Centenary of the ANC' (30 March 2007).
54 ANC, 'Organisational Renewal' (10 April 2012), 60.
55 Ibid.
56 ANC, '53rd National Conference: Resolutions' (31 January 2013), 8.
57 The theory of colonialism of a special type as originally hypothesised in 1962 was that the black population experienced oppression first and foremost on the basis of their race, and that there existed no acute divisions within the African population itself.
58 ANC, 'Organisational Renewal' (10 April 2012), 3.
59 Ibid., 60.
60 Ibid., 44.
61 Ibid.
62 Ibid.
63 Ibid.
64 Ibid., 3, 44.
65 African National Congress (ANC), 'Legislature and Governance', Policy Discussion Document (March 2012), www.anc.org.za.
66 ANC, 'Organisational Renewal' (10 April 2012), 44.
67 Ibid., 7, 23, 29.
68 Ibid., 44.
69 Y. Carrim, 'Bridging the gap between the ideas and practice: Challenges of the new local government system', *Umrabulo* 10, 1 (2001).
70 ANC, 'Organisational Renewal' (10 April 2012), 44.
71 J. Steinberg, 'A place for civics in a democratic polity? The fate of local institutions of resistance after apartheid', in G. Adler and J. Steinberg (eds), *From Comrades to Citizens: The South Africa Civics Movement and the Transition to Democracy* (Basingstoke, 2000), 190.
72 On intolerance of alternative political traditions in local decision-making structures in Kwazakele in the Eastern Cape, see J. Cherry, 'Hegemony, democracy and civil society: Political participation in Kwazakele Township, 1980–93', in Adler and Steinberg, *From Comrades to Citizens*, 106–107. On the arbitrary application of punishment in the popular justice of 'people's courts', see also B. Bozzoli, *Theatres of Struggle and the End of Apartheid* (Johannesburg, 2004), 141, 149–156.
73 S. Mufson, *Fighting Years: Black Resistance and the Struggle for a New South Africa* (Boston, 1990),

129–130.
74 African National Congress, '50th National Conference: Resolutions' (22 December 1997).
75 ANC, 'Report of the Commission on Organisational Renewal' (30 June 2007).
76 ANC, '53rd National Conference: Resolutions' (31 January 2013), 4.
77 Ibid., 5.
78 See ANC 'Organisational Renewal' (10 April 2012), 31–33; and ANC, '53rd National Conference: Resolutions' (31 January 2013).
79 See ANC, '53rd National Conference: Resolutions' (31 January 2013), 5.
80 ANC 'Organisational Renewal' (10 April 2012), 29.
81 Ibid., 30; and ANC, '53rd National Conference: Resolutions' (31 January 2013), 9.
82 For detail on the proposals and identified challenges, see Chapter 6 the ANC's 'Organisational Renewal' report (10 April 2012), entitled 'Building a Contingent of Conscious, Competent, Conscientious and Disciplined Cadres'.
83 ANC, 'ANC: People's Movement and Agent for Change' (1 July 2000).
84 ANC, 'Towards the Centenary of the ANC' (30 March 2007).
85 *Daily Maverick*, 'Mangaung: On organisational renewal, ANC talks the talk', 20.12.2012, www.dailymaverick.co.za/article/2012-12-20-mangaung-on-organisational-renewal-anc-talks-the-talk/#.U5bo6Sjm6dl; *New Age*, 'Renewal: ANC optimistic', 21.12.2012, www.thenewage.co.za/75009-1111-53-Renewal_ANC_optimistic.
86 *City Press*, 'Corruption: ANC's new integrity commission has powers to dismiss', 20.12.2012, www.citypress.co.za/politics/corruption-ancs-new-integrity-commission-has-powers-to-dismiss/; *Political Bureau*, 'We need new breed of cadres – Makhura', 11.04.2012, www.iol.co.za/news/politics/we-need-new-breed-of-cadres-makhura-1.1273385?showComments=true#.U5bR_yjm6dl.
87 *Business Day*, 'ANC launches its political school', 12.08.2012, www.bdlive.co.za/national/politics/2012/08/12/anc-launches-its-political-school.
88 *Mail & Guardian*, 'Mbalula: "hereditary approach" will lose elections', 28.09.2012, http://mg.co.za/article/2012-09-28-00-mbalula-hereditary-approach-will-lose-elections.
89 *Daily Maverick*, 22.08.2012, 'Malema and the disciplinary committee: A rough guide', www.dailymaverick.co.za/article/2011-08-22-malema-and-the-disciplinary-commission-a-rough-guide#.U5m2uCjm6dk.
90 *Sowetan*, 'ANC adopts policies to address weaknesses', 20.12.2012, www.sowetanlive.co.za/news/2012/12/20/anc-adopts-policies-to-address-weaknesses.
91 ANC, 'ANC 53rd National Conference Programme', 16–20 December 2012, www.anc.org.za/docs/introtxt/2012/programmey.pdf.
92 *Sunday Independent*, 'Malema is reckless – Mbalula', 16.06.2013, www.iol.co.za/news/special-features/malema-is-reckless-mbalula-1.1533057#.U5mICyjm6dk.
93 ANC, 'Organisational Renewal' (10 April 2012), 29.
94 Thanks are due to Anthony Butler for alerting me to the struggle within the ANC to assert control over a new generation of cadres.
95 ANC, 'Organisational Renewal' (10 April 2012), 27–28.
96 Ibid., 30.
97 *City Press*, 'Ruling party plans to build its own school of politics', 28.04.2012, www.citypress.co.za/politics/ruling-party-plans-to-build-its-own-school-of-politics-20120428/; *ANC Today*, vol. 12, 45, 'Central to the ANC renewal is training and educating the member', Readers Forum: November 2012, www.anc.org.za/docs/anctoday/2012/at45.htm#art3.
98 *SABC News*, 'Key issues to be considered by the ANC on issues of renewal', 11.04.2012, www.sabc.co.za/news/a/8fa500804ad8b30e97bdd75553dc7d93/Key-issues-to-be-considered-by-

the-ANC-on-issues-of-renewal-20121104.
99 ANC, '53rd National Conference: Resolutions' (31 January 2013), 5; see also *Umrabulo*, 'The meaning of a cadre', 1st Quarter (2013) on the qualities of a cadre versus a member.
100 ANC 'Organisational Renewal' (10 April 2012), 47.
101 Ibid., 30.
102 V. Darraq, 'Being a "movement of the people" and a governing party: Study of the African National Congress mass character', *Journal of Southern African Studies* 34, 2 (2008), 429–449.
103 M. Duverger, *Political Parties: Their Organisation and Activity in the Modern State* (London, 1964 [1954]), 63; Darraq, 'Being a "movement of the people"', 430.
104 Booysen, *The African National Congress*.
105 On the limitations of exclusively 'organisational' or 'sociological' classifications of parties, see R. Gunther and L. Diamond, 'Species of political parties: A new typology', *Party Politics* 9, 2 (2003), 169–170.
106 ANC 'Organisational Renewal' (10 April 2012), 50.
107 Prevost (2006) and Johnson (2002), both cited in Booysen, *The African National Congress*, 92.
108 ANC 'Organisational Renewal' (10 April 2012), 18.
109 E. Mandel, 'Vanguard parties', *Mid-American Review of Sociology* 8, 2 (1983), 1, 13.
110 ANC, 'Organisational Renewal' (10 April 2012), 14.
111 On the topic of a united front, see the ANC's reference to the 'three key features of a progressive movement for national liberation or social emancipation', which includes adopting a broad church character: 'Unlike a tightly knit organisation, a movement promotes united front politics among the broadly like-minded forces and formations' (ANC, 'Organisational Renewal' (10 April 2012), 22).
112 Although this chapter does not see the typology of the class-based 'Leninist Party' as defined by Gunther and Diamond as applying to the ANC, their article does provide a useful categorisation of types of mass party and their varying characteristics (Gunther and Diamond, 'Species of political parties').
113 Southall, *Liberation Movements in Power*, 322.
114 Cosatu, 'Organisational Renewal' (2012), 7.
115 *Business Day*, 12 August 2012.
116 *Business Day*, 'ANC's political school may finally have found a home', 10.07.2013, www.bdlive.co.za/national/politics/2013/07/10/ancs-political-school-may-finally-have-found-a-home.

Chapter 10
1 E. Friedman and J. Wong (eds), *Political Transitions in Dominant Party Systems: Learning to Lose* (New York, 2008), 9.
2 R. Michels, *Political Parties: A Sociological Study of the Oligarchical Tendencies of Modern Democracy* (New York, 1915).
3 M. Duverger, *Political Parties: Their Organization and Activity in the Modern State* (London, 1959); A. Panebianco, *Political Parties: Organization and Power* (Cambridge, 1988); I. Van Biezen, (2003) *Political Parties in New Democracies* (New York, 2003); P. Mair, *Party System Change: Approaches and Interpretations* (Oxford 1997).
4 R. Harmel and K. Janda, 'An integrated theory of party goals and party change', *Journal of Theoretical Politics* 6, 3 (1994), 259–287.
5 The key documents include ANC, 'Organisational democracy and discipline in the movement', *Umrabulo* 3 (1997); ANC, 'Challenges of the leadership in the current phase:

Discussion document for the ANC national conference', *Umrabulo* 3 (1997); ANC, 'Through the eye of a needle: Choosing the best cadres to lead transformation', *Umrabulo* 11 (2001). For analysis, see A.M. Butler, 'How democratic is the African National Congress', *Journal of Southern African Studies* 31, 4 (2005), 719–736.
6   ANC, *Political Report to the 53rd National Conference of the ANC* (Johannesburg, 2012).
7   ANC, *Organisational Report of the National Executive Committee to the 53rd National Conference* (Johannesburg, 2012), 3.1.1.
8   Ibid.
9   ANC, *Secretary General's Organisational Report: ANC National General Council* (Johannesburg, 2005).
10 See A.M. Butler (ed.), *Paying for Politics* (Auckland Park, 2010).
11 J. Netshitenzhe, 'Competing identities of a national liberation movement and the challenges of incumbency', *ANC Today* 12, 23 (2012).
12 ANC, 'The Investigating Task Team on list and other disputes', Unpublished document (2012).
13 Ibid., 13.
14 Ibid., 2.
15 Constitutional Court, Case CCT 109/12 [2012] ZACC 31. Heard on 20 November 2012 and 29 November 2012. Orders granted 21 November 2012 and 14 December 2012. Reasons for judgment 18 December 2012, section 46.
16 Ibid.
17 Ibid., section 90.
18 Selective recruitment and exclusion largely revolve around branch processes because of the role assigned to them by the ANC's constitution. Ninety per cent of conference delegates come from branches and they are elected at 'properly constituted branch general meetings'. The number of delegates should be broadly proportional to paid-up memberships, with each branch 'in good standing' entitled to at least one delegate. The remainder of the voting delegates at the conference are allocated by the NEC 'from among members of the Provincial Executive Committees, the ANC Veterans' League, the ANC Youth League and the ANC Women's League'. ANC, *African National Congress Constitution: Amended and Adopted at the 52nd National Conference, Polokwane* (Johannesburg, African National Congress, 2007), 10–11.
19 A variety of explanations of local protest actions have been advanced. See, for example, P. Alexander, 'Rebellion of the poor: South Africa's service delivery protests – a preliminary analysis', *Review of African Political Economy* 37, 123 (2010), 25–40; K. von Holdt, 'South Africa: The transition to violent democracy', *Review of African Political Economy* 40, 138 (2013), 589–604.
20 ANC, *Towards the Centenary of the ANC: Discussion Document on Organisational Review: A Strategic Agenda for Organisational Renewal* (Johannesburg, 2007).
21 ANC, *Organisational Report of the National Executive Committee to the 53rd National Conference by Secretary General, Gwede Mantashe* (Johannesburg, 2012), 3.1.1.
22 ANC, *53rd National Conference Resolutions* (Johannesburg, African National Congress, 2013), 5–6.
23 ANC, 'Statement of the National Executive Committee on the occasion of the 100th anniversary of the ANC', *ANC Today* 13, 1 (Johannesburg, 2012).
24 H.H. Pedersen, 'What do parties want? Policy versus office', *West European Politics* 35, 4 (2012), 896–910.
25 A.M. Butler, *The Idea of the ANC* (Auckland Park, 2012).
26 Pedersen, 'What do parties want'.

27 C. Forestiere and C.S. Allen, 'The formation of cognitive locks in single party dominant regimes', *International Political Science Review* 32, 4 (2011), 380–395.
28 Most recently, F. Boucek, 'The maintenance and decline of dominant party systems in the developed words: Inter- and intra-party interpretations', Paper presented at a Dominant Party Systems Conference at the University of Michigan, 9–10 May 2014, 3; more fully, F. Boucek, *Factional Politics: How Dominant Parties Implode or Stabilize* (New York, 2012).

Index

adaptation 1, 6–8, 10, 30–4, 89–90, 136, 158, 166, 168; *see also* party change
African National Congress (ANC) 1–6, 11–13, 101–20, 120–36, 137–56, 157–68
Anwar Ibrahim 57
apartheid 114–16, 118, 155, 160
Arias Solís, Cristóbal 48

Badawi, Abdullah Ahmad 58
Barisan Alternatif (BA) 61–2
Barisan Nasional (BN) 52, 54, 58, 60–3, 64, 66–7
Bittar, Jacó 71
Brazil 8, 9, 11, 69–83, 157
Brazilian Communist Party (PCB) 71, 73
Brazilian Democratic Movement (MDB) 71, 77–82
Brazilian Labour Party (PTB) 71
Brazilian Republican Party (PRB) 81
BRICS group 8, 82
Brizola, Leonel 73–4
Building a New Brazil (CNB) 77–8
Bukhary, Syed Mokhtar al- 64
Bumiputera Commercial and Industrial Community (BCIC) 56

Calderón, Felipe 48
Calles, Plutarco Elías 35
Cárdenas, Cuauhtémoc 39, 47–8
Cardoso, Fernando Henrique 73
Carrim, Yunus 148

Central Standing Committee (Taiwan) 17, 22
Chen Shui-ban 20
Chiang Ching-kuo 17–18
Chikane, Frank 131, 134
China 17–19, 26, 84–100, 115
Chinese Communist Party; *see* Communist Party of China
Chinese Propaganda Department 85–6
Communist Party of Brazil (PC do B) 73
Communist Party of China (CPC) 8, 11, 17, 84–100, 151, 157, 160
Congress of South African Trade Unions (Cosatu) 8, 116, 118, 138, 142–3, 155, 159
Congress of the People (Cope) 117
corruption 12, 21, 29, 49, 59, 61–5, 86–7, 93–9, 101, 103, 105, 116–17, 122, 134, 140
Cronin, Jeremy 130

Daim Zainuddin 57
Democratic Action Party (DAP) 61, 62, 64
Democratic Alliance (DA) 6
Democratic Labour Party (PDT) 73
Democratic Progressive Party (DPP) 19, 20, 25
Democrats (DEM) 78
Deng Xiaoping 91, 98
Dirceu, José 76
Dlamini-Zuma, Nkosazana 161
dominant parties 1–6, 29–37, 101–19, 135, 165–8
Dutra, Olívio 71

Economic Freedom Fighters (EFF) 151, 159–60
elections 1–2, 4, 7, 9–17, 20–4, 32, 36, 39, 41–6, 70–5, 78–83, 104, 108–10, 160–2, 167

factionalism 8, 10–13, 15–16, 25, 27, 28, 44–9, 57–70, 101–20, 140, 143, 149, 158–67
Fox, Vicente 21
France 19, 25–6
Freedom Charter 115

Gandhi, Indira 107, 111–13, 119
Gandhi, Mahatma 107, 110
Gauteng province 1, 150
Genoino, José 75
Ghana 125, 128, 133–4
Giri, V.V. 112–13

Hamzah, Razaleigh 60
Harmel, R. 8, 15, 16, 27
Hayek, Friedrich 54
Holomisa, Bantu 116

India 29, 66, 101–20
Indian National Congress (INC) 5, 12, 101–20
Institutional Revolutionary Party (PRI) 5, 6, 10, 29–51
Internet 12, 84–100
Italy 2, 5, 29, 104

Janda, K., 8, 15, 16, 27
Japan 2, 5, 29, 104
Jasmine Revolution 85

Kabwe conference 123–4, 126, 131–2, 135, 149
King Pu-tsung 24
Kripalani, J.B. 110
Kuomintang (KMT) 5, 6, 9, 14–28
KwaZulu-Natal 162–3

Lee Teng-hui 18, 22
Leninism 17, 26, 74, 91, 154
Lien Chan 18, 20–2
Liu Tienan 87

Lula da Silva, Luiz Inácio 9, 69–70, 71–4, 76–7, 79–80
Luo Changping 87
Luxembourg 29

Ma Ying-jeou 18, 21, 23, 25
Mafikeng conference 123–4
Mahathir Mohamad 56
Majority Sector 76–7
Makhura, David 150
Malaysia 5, 10, 52–68
Malema, Julius 150–1
Mandela, Nelson 29, 103–4, 108, 116
Mangaung conference 132, 137, 139, 155, 161, 163
Mantashe, Gwede 130, 160–1, 164
Marxism 71, 75, 115, 154
Mashatile, Paul 150
Mass Democratic Movement (MDM) 142, 144–5
Mbalula, Fikile 150–1
Mbeki, Thabo 112, 116–19, 131, 134, 139–40, 155, 162–4
Mensalão scandal 77
Mexico, 5, 6, 10, 29–51
Michoacán state 47, 48–9
mixed member majoritarian system 20, 26, 28
Mojapelo, Paul 150
Monreal Ávila, Ricardo 48–9
Morogoro conference 115, 142
Motlanthe, Kgalema 131
Movement of Landless Workers (MST) 82
multi-party system 2, 47, 71

Najib Razak 58–9, 64–6, 67–8
National Action Party (PAN) 32
National Democratic Revolution (NDR) 135, 136, 146, 153
National Deployment Committee (NDC) 130–1
National Executive Committee (NEC) 11, 117–18, 131, 138
national liberation movements 3–4, 102, 119, 155
National Party 121, 124
Nehru, Jawaharlal 104, 108, 110–3, 115
neoliberalism 53–5, 58–9, 70, 140

New Economic Model 59, 65
New Economic Policy (NEP) 55–6
North American Free Trade Agreement (NAFTA) 41

Olvera, Marco Antonio 48
organisational renewal 137–56

Pakatan Rakyat (PR) 52, 64–7
Paraguay 29–30
Parti Islam SeMalaysia (PAS) 60–3, 64, 66, 67
Parti Keadilan Nasional 61–2, 64
Partido dos Trabalhadores *see* Workers' Party of Brazil
party change 8, 9, 14–16, 28, 34, 158; *see also* adaptation
party dominance *see* dominant parties
Party of Brazilian Social Democracy (PSDB) 73, 77–8, 82
Party of the Democratic Revolution (PRD) 32, 47–8
Party Socialism and Freedom (PSOL) 76, 77–8
Patel, Sardar 104, 109–10, 112
Peemedebisation 77–8, 83
Peña Nieto, Enrique 33
People's Daily 87, 89, 91, 94
Peru 50
Plan Real 73
Polokwane conference 112, 117, 131, 163
Potgieter-Gqubule, Febe 150
PRONASOL 40

Radical Democracy 76
Reconstruction and Development Programme (RDP) 117–18
Reddy, Sanjiva 112–13
Revolutionary Communist Party (PRC) 75
Rousseff, Dilma 69–70, 77, 80

Salinas, Carlos 39–42, 27
São Paulo 71, 73, 75–6, 81
Senegal 29
Shaik, Schabir 117

single non-transferable vote (SNTV) system 20, 26, 28
small- and medium-scale enterprises (SMEs) 56, 58, 63
Socialist Democracy (DS) 76–7, 82
Soong, James 20
South Africa 2–13, 101–68
South African Communist Party (SACP) 116, 118, 142, 151, 159
Southall, Roger 3–4, 135, 141, 155
Sweden 2, 29
Syndicate 107, 112–13

Taib Mahmud 64
Taiwan 5, 6, 9, 14–28, 29, 30
Taiwan Solidarity Union (TSU) 19
Tambo, O.R. 115
Tinoco Rubí, Víctor Manuel 48
tripartite alliance 11, 118, 139, 142–3, 144, 148, 159

United Democratic Front (UDF) 115
United Democratic Movement (UDM) 116
United Kingdom 2
United Malays National Organisation (UMNO) 5, 10–11, 52–68
United Progressive Alliance 113
United States of America 2, 18, 24, 26, 85

Walesa, Lech 29
Weibo 86–90, 92–6, 99–100
Workers' Party of Brazil (PT) 8–9, 11, 69–83, 157

Xi Jinping 87
Xue, Charles 93

Zacatecas state 48–9
Zedillo, Ernesto 41, 42
Zhu Xinhua 87, 93
Zimbabwe 3
Zuma, Jacob 103–4, 117, 134, 139–40, 151, 155, 163, 165